SACRED

QUEST

ALSO BY DOUG BANISTER

The Word and Power Church

SACRED QUEST

QUEST

DISCOVERING SPIRITUAL INTIMACY WITH GOD

DOUG BANISTER

ZondervanPublishingHouse

Grand Rapids, Michigan

A Division of HarperCollinsPublishers

Sacred Quest
Copyright © 2001 by Douglas Banister
Requests for information should be addressed to:

⚒Zondervan Publishing House

Grand Rapids, Michigan 49530

Library of Congress Cataloging-in-Publication Data

Banister, Doug, 1961–
    Sacred quest : discovering spiritual intimacy with God / Doug Banister.
       p.   cm.
    Includes bibliographical references.
    ISBN 0–310–22833–6
    1. Christian life—Pentecostal authors.   2. Spiritual life—Case studies.   I. Title.
BV4501.2 .B38235 2001
248.4—dc21

00-051262
CIP

This edition printed on acid-free paper.

All Scripture quotations, unless otherwise noted, are taken from the *Holy Bible: New International Version*®. Copyright © 1973, 1978, 1984 by International Bible Society. Used by permission of Zondervan Publishing House. All rights reserved.

Scripture quotations identified as *The Message* are from Eugene H. Peterson, *The Message: The New Testament in Contemporary English* (Colorado Springs: NavPress, 1993).

All rights reserved. No part of this publication may be reproduced, stored in a retrieval system, or transmitted in any form or by any means—electronic, mechanical, photocopy, recording, or any other—except for brief quotations in printed reviews, without the prior permission of the publisher.

Published in association with the literary agency of Alive Communications, Inc., 7680 Goddard Street, Suite 200, Colorado Springs, CO 80920.

Interior design by Melissa Elenbaas

Printed in the United States of America

---

01 02 03 04 05 06 07 08 /❖DC/ 10 9 8 7 6 5 4 3 2 1

FOR BRYDEN, HUNTER,

SAJEN AND ASHTEN:

MAY YOU QUEST WELL

CONTENTS

PROLOGUE

My son and I love to read stories about the Quest. (The girls like stories about horses.) Hunter and I often end our evenings questing, especially in the winter months when night comes early and there are no fireflies to catch or baseballs to throw. One of our favorite quest stories is *The Hobbit*.

"We shall soon before the break of day start on our long journey," the dwarf-warrior Thorin tells a bewildered Bilbo Baggins in the first chapter of J. R. R. Tolkien's legendary tale of one hobbit's great adventure. It is "a journey from which some of us, or perhaps all of us ... may never return. It is a solemn moment."[1]

Bilbo, a comfortable, well-to-do hobbit who had never taken a risk in his life, finds himself running after Thorin and his fellow dwarves as they begin their spectacular adventure. "To the end of his days Bilbo could never remember how he found himself outside, without a hat, walking stick or any money, or anything that he usually took when we went out, leaving his second breakfast half-finished and quite unwashed up, pushing his keys into Gandalf's hands and running as fast as his furry feet could carry him down his lane."[2]

We soon find that Bilbo and his companions are in search of vast treasure buried deep beneath a faraway mountain. But the quest is about a lot more than a treasure hunt. Bilbo is restless and dissatisfied with his life. He enjoys his comfortable, pipe-smoking, risk-free existence in his well-decorated hobbit hole. Yet he knows he is made for more than this. Thorin's invitation to begin a perilous but rewarding quest captures

Bilbo's heart. When the quest ends, he has discovered much more than treasure. He has discovered the secret to a fulfilled life.

The quest complete, a much different hobbit returns to his comfortable home under The Hill. "Though few believed any of his tales," Tolkien tells us, "he remained very happy to the end of his days, and those were extraordinarily long."[3] True happiness, we learn, belongs only to those who complete their quest.

Why are so many of the world's most beloved stories about great quests? Tales about questing come down to us from every culture and every age: Homer's *Odyssey*, King Arthur's Quest for the Holy Grail, John Bunyan's *Pilgrim's Progress*, George Lucas's *Star Wars* trilogy. Why do we love these stories so, and why do they embed themselves in the deep places of our psyche?

We love questing stories because life itself is a Quest. The journey metaphor matches the contours of our own inner worlds. We know that life is a long journey and that some finish the journey well, some finish poorly, and some never really begin at all. Christians know that the spiritual life is the greatest quest of all. Our sacred quest begins when a gospel-bearing Thorin thunders into our own cozy little world and summons us to set forth on a dangerous but irresistible spiritual journey from which we may never return.

The object of our sacred quest is not a holy grail or a pile of treasure, but the ultimate prize of knowing Jesus Christ intimately. The restlessness we feel, the dissatisfaction with the emptiness of life, the ache for something more—these are not a cruel joke played on us by our treacherous hearts. These whispers of our hearts are invitations to quest. They warn us of the dangers of settling for a warm hobbit hole when we know we are made for much more. The hauntings of a restless heart summon us to continue the Quest until the heart's most passionate longings are finally satisfied in the embrace of Christ.

We who respond to the call of Christ and bid farewell to our comfortable worlds, out of breath and with our second breakfast half eaten, will face our own dragons and goblins along the way. All the powers of hell are unleashed against the weary pilgrim who steadfastly presses forward in the sacred quest of knowing Jesus Christ. There are betrayals and battles, disappointments and dangers, false starts and tumbles into dark ravines. How do we keep going? The true happiness we all long for only comes to those who stay on the path and don't look back. This is a book for people who want to finish the Quest well.

Great quest stories often require the adventurers to solve riddles before continuing on their journey. Bilbo cannot pass by the miserable creature Gollum and continue his quest until he first unravels Gollum's mysterious riddle. There are riddles to be solved on the sacred quest as well. What are they? How do we solve them? This book explores four riddles of spiritual intimacy (identified in chapter 3) that must be resolved for the Quest to continue.

No one quests alone in these stories, and we won't either. Some of the most memorable moments in questing tales happen when the travelers stop for the night and warm one another with a good fire and their own stories. I have chosen to include many stories from fellow pilgrims in this book. I hope these stories warm your heart and encourage you along the way.

The heroes of the great quests are often helped on their journey by wise guides who have gone before them. Bilbo is mentored by the wizard Gandalf. Luke Skywalker would never have made it through the first *Star Wars* film if not for the help of Obee Won Kenobee.

Who will guide us on our sacred quest? There are many different streams of Christian spirituality, and each one has much to teach us about solving the riddles of spiritual intimacy. I have sought out spiritual directors from the charismatic and evangelical traditions for this book because these are the spiritual streams that have most shaped my own spiritual journey.

This book was a struggle for me to write because it became intensely personal. My own sacred quest has had its share of setbacks. Like Bilbo, I have often wanted to turn from the Quest and run back to the comfort of where I began, or settle for a counterfeit treasure that is no substitute for the real thing.

The first drafts of the book avoided the rugged terrain of my own heart and hid behind too many quotes of great saints who had quested well in the past. I am thankful to my wife, Sandi, my friends Jim and

Leanne Dickson, and my editor, John Sloan, for urging me to let the story of my sacred quest mingle with yours in the pages of this book.

I would like to thank Dave Russel, Kathy Tarr, Rick and Theresa Dunn, Janey Tolliver, and Jeff Townsend for their help along the way. Thanks as well to the Blackberry Farm family and the Smee family for giving me sacred places to think and write about the sacred quest.

Most of all, I want to thank my wife, Sandi, in whose love I experience the love of Christ.

WHEN WE FAIL TO
BOND WITH GOD

Brian half-heartedly poked the last glowing ember in the fireplace, took another sip of cold coffee, and leaned back into a tired couch.[1]

"I've just about given up hope," he said, unable to make eye contact. "If my wife finds out I've been looking at pornography again on the Internet, I'm afraid she's going to pack up and take the kids back to Detroit." We were alone in the great room of a retreat center where I had been speaking. Dew gathered on the windows. Everyone else had gone to bed hours before.

"I've tried everything," Brian sighed. "I've fasted for twenty-one days. I've been prayed for. I've asked guys to hold me accountable, but I just can't . . ." Brian's voice trailed off into painful silence.

"What happens when you struggle?" I asked.

"I struggle most when I'm really stressed out. Our law practice has had a lousy year, and the senior partners are really driving us to bill more hours. And Becky and I have been fighting a lot. I just want to get away. Sometimes when I'm driving home from work, I have this wild fantasy to get on the interstate and drive until I hit Wyoming."

"But you know you can't do that, so you wind up on the Net instead?"

"I suppose so. I've even found a way around the cyber block on our computer. I feel helpless. Before I know it, I'm looking at stuff I know I shouldn't be looking at."

Later that weekend I asked Brian to describe his relationship with his father.

"A pretty good man," he replied.

I asked Brian if I could pray for him, specifically to ask the Holy Spirit to reveal any memories about his father that might help him understand his bondage to pornography.

"I guess so . . . sure."

Within seconds, pictures from Brian's childhood began to drift across his mind. Brian described them to me as if he were watching a movie inside his head.

"I've just come home from college—I was a freshman at Michigan State . . . been away a long time. My dad is in the living room, watching the Friday night movie. . . . He lifts a hand, but doesn't get up."

Brian paused, visibly shaken, reliving the painful memory. "I guess the movie is more important than I am."

The Spirit continued to gently reveal a scrapbook of memories long since packed away in the attic of Brian's heart. The themes are all the same: a son desperate for his father's love and approval never finds it. Brian sat quietly on the bed for a long time.

"God built you for relationship, Brian," I began. "You were created to connect with God and other people. Sometimes psychologists call this bonding. In a healthy home, a son bonds with his father. The father then shows the son how to bond with the heavenly Father."

"That didn't happen."

"You're right. But you still have needs. We can't function without an intimate relationship with God. When this need for intimacy wasn't met the way God intended, you began to seek intimacy in other places."

"Are you saying that my struggle with pornography is really about my relationship with God?" Brian asked, a puzzled look on his face.

"Yes," I replied. "Most problems usually are."

BUILT FOR INTIMACY

Everyone seeks intimacy with God. Ignore this need and you end up where Brian did—looking for God in the wrong place. God designed us to bond relationally with himself. All of us are on a lifelong quest to know him more intimately. We *must* learn how to bond with him if we are to become the people he has called us to be.

The cost of failing to bond with God can be staggering. Addiction, low self-esteem, depression, religiosity, burnout, and relational problems are just several consequences of failing to bond intimately with God. I know. Mishandling my own desires for intimacy nearly cost me my ministry. I will tell you more about my own pilgrimage in the next chapter. Much of what I have learned about intimacy has come from my own painful quest to bond with God. For now, let's consider what the Bible has to say about the critical importance of intimate bonding with our Creator.

SPIRITUAL BONDING

The God of Scripture is a relational God. The three members of the Trinity—God the Father, God the Son, and God the Spirit—exist in relationship together. Jesus describes their relationship as intensely intimate. Jesus says to the Father, "You are in me and I am in you."[2]

The God of Scripture is a relational God.

The creation story is an account of a relational God creating a man and a woman he could bond with relationally. We find a clue about the relational heart of God when we read, "Let us make man in *our* image, in *our* likeness."[3] God, who exists in relationship, creates men and women who bear this same relational likeness.

God did not create just one human being, but two. When Adam was the only person in the universe, God said, "It is not good for the man to be alone."[4] Why isn't it? Was relationship with God not enough for him? Evidently not. Adam needed to be in relationship with God *and* in relationship with other people. This is why Jesus sums up all the teaching of Scripture in two simple commands: love God and love our neighbor. "Relationship, or bonding, then, is at the foundation of God's nature," writes Christian psychologist Henry Cloud. "Since we are created in his likeness, relationship is our most fundamental need, the very foundation of who we are. Without relationship, without attachment to God and others, we can't be our true selves. We can't be truly human."[5]

If you fail to bond with other people, you rob yourself of the nutrients you need to grow as a person. A study in 1945 plotted the long-term health of babies in state institutions. The physical needs of all the boys and girls were met; however, only some of the babies were held, caressed, and talked to because too few nurses were available to hold all the infants. The researchers found that the children who had not been held became ill much more frequently and had a much higher death rate. Their emotional development slowed down or even stopped.[6]

Relationships are important to adults as well. Over the past twelve years I have noticed that some people in our church change and grow, while others do not. Without fail, the most common difference between the two kinds of people is their willingness to commit to authentic relationships with a handful of other people. People who give the gift of their heart to others grow. People who won't, don't. My pastoral counsel to Brian as we left one another that weekend was to find some fellow pilgrims struggling with similar issues who would walk with him in his quest for healing.

As important as bonding with good friends is, however, it is not enough. We must bond with God as well. Connecting with God at an intimate level is even more difficult than connecting intimately with our friends. The consequences of failing to bond with God can be even more destructive than when we fail to bond with people. Just as those infants suffered and died physically and emotionally because of the lack of human touch, our souls wither and rot when we do not know how to touch and be touched by Jesus Christ in a deep and personal way.

Many excellent books have been written about the all-important need to bond with others. My heart in this book is to explore with you the equally important developmental task of bonding with God.

Jesus taught us that the very source of our spiritual life is our friendship with him.

"I am the Real Vine and my Father is the Farmer. . . .

"Live in me. Make your home in me just as I do in you. In the same way that a branch can't bear grapes by itself but only by being joined to the vine, you can't bear fruit unless you are joined with me.

"I am the Vine, you are the branches. When you are joined with me and I with you, the relation intimate and organic, the harvest is sure to be abundant. Separated, you can't produce a thing. Anyone who separates from me is deadwood, gathered up and thrown on the bonfire."[7]

Let's explore what happens when we fail to bond with God.

ADDICTION

Brian is addicted to sex. Bonding with others will help. But even the best friendships cannot bear the weight of another person's need for God. Addiction occurs when our legitimate need to bond intimately with God is bent and we begin to seek intimate connections in illegitimate ways. When the behavior becomes habitual and compulsive, we are hooked.

God describes addictive behavior among his people when he laments, "My people have committed two sins: They have forsaken me, the spring of living water, and have dug their own cisterns, broken cisterns that cannot hold water."[8] We are designed to drink deeply from the pure water that flows out of relationship with God. Foolishly, we turn away from these pure, life-giving waters to broken, muddy wells that leak and poison us.

"We are all addicts, in every sense of the word," psychologist Gerald May writes. "Addiction to alcohol and other drugs are simply more obvious and tragic addictions than others have. . . . Addictions are not limited to substances. I was also addicted to work, performance, responsibility, intimacy, being liked, helping others, and an almost endless list of other behaviors."[9]

All of life is spiritual, and all of life is a quest for God. Any compulsive behavior that I cannot control is an addiction—a counterfeit search for intimate connection.

Another word for bonding is "attachment." It comes from the old French word attaché, which means "nailed to." God designed us to be "nailed to" him. Misplaced attachment nails our longings to specific objects and creates addiction.[10]

"I was filling the hole in my heart with food."

Jackie's failure to bond with God resulted in an eating disorder. "I'd been overweight all my life," Jackie says. "I did everything to lose the weight. I did Slim Fast, Weight Watchers, a 1200-calorie diet, the cabbage soup diet, herb pills—I was desperate. When I began having kids, my weight went over two hundred pounds."

Jackie heard about a Weigh Down Workshop at church and signed up. She began to understand that she was hungry for more than just food. "I was turning to food for comfort—when I felt lonely or depressed," she recalls. "I had a hole in my heart, and I was trying to fill it with food." Today, seventy-five pounds lighter, Jackie has learned the difference between soul hunger and physical hunger. "I found out that if I wanted to change, I had to start seeking him."

"I was trying to escape the emptiness."

Michael, a real-estate developer, fought narcotics addiction for seven years, dragging his wife and two children through hell in the process. "The hardest thing about being an addict is not knowing why or how you have fallen into such a hopeless and helpless state," Michael says. "I had a loving wife, two children and one on the way, yet every day after work I found myself feasting on a handful of narcotics trying to escape the pain of years of emptiness and searching."

After one all-night drug binge, Michael finally "cried out to God in what I thought was my last chance." God answered his prayers through the phone call of a friend, who invited Michael to attend an early morning Promise Keepers men's Bible study. Michael had often attended church, but had never begun a personal relationship with Jesus Christ and had never experienced relational intimacy with God and others as he did in this small group. He finally found what he had been looking for—an intimate friendship with Jesus. The power of bonding with God and others far surpassed the power of his addiction. "It transformed a despairing young man into a devoted disciple of Jesus Christ," Michael says.

Not every addiction is conquered as dramatically as Jackie's and Michael's. Old patterns of desire and idolatrous fulfillment don't die easily. Brian's journey is still in progress. So is my own. At the core of every addiction is a legitimate longing to bond with God. When we ignore that longing, or "nail it" to a lesser god, we bring great pain upon ourselves, to our loved ones, and to our Lord.

Low Self-esteem

Failing to bond with God can also cause low self-esteem. Most Christians know intellectually that God loves them, but we must also *experience* this intimate love in our own souls. When our daily experience of God's love lags behind the knowledge of it, we begin to doubt God: "If he really is who he says he is, then why don't I feel his love?" Or we doubt ourselves: "I must not be worthy of love since I rarely experience God's affection toward me."

Healthy self-esteem is more than believing certain facts about ourselves. Healthy self-esteem is *knowing* that we are loved because we have tasted intimacy with the One Who Is Love. Imagine a little girl whose parents are away on a long trip. They have been away so long she can't remember them. All she knows is that her nanny says Mom and Dad love her very much. When the little girl gets lonely, the nanny brings out some old letters from her parents that tell her how much they love her. After a while, the lonely little girl doubts that her mother and father actually wrote the letters. If they really love her, she reasons, they would come back and get to know her again. And she would be right.

> **M**ost Christians know intellectually that God loves them, but we must also *experience* this intimate love in our own souls.

In a similar way, we need present-tense encounters with our living Lord to reaffirm the truths we read in his letters. Self-esteem is a blend of biblical truth and present experience. Failing to bond with God intimately robs us of the daily awareness of our "belovedness" in Christ and reinforces a dangerous gap between what God says and what we experience.

Depression

Monica, a thirty-eight-year-old mother of three boys, has a gift of sincere encouragement, seemingly boundless energy, and a bright, sunny smile. One night, Monica stunned her small group by sharing with them that beneath her peppy veneer hid a draining battle with depression.

The author of Psalm 42 expresses the pain depressed people often feel: "My tears have been my food day and night," the writer laments. "My soul is downcast within me." His isolation from God invokes a cry that has become one of devotional literature's most passionate pleas for intimacy with the Lord: "As the deer pants for streams of water, so my soul pants for you, O God. My soul thirsts for God, for the living God. Where can I go and meet with God?" But even in his pain, he knows the source of healing: "Put your hope in God," he tells his soul. "For I will yet praise him, my Savior and my God."

Long before anyone had invented the word "psychology" this ancient songwriter had grasped the spiritual dynamics of depression—a lack of intimacy with God. Of course, not all depression is spiritually based,[11] but often depression has more to do with our souls than our bodies. Joy is one of the fruits of a life lived in vital connection with God, what Scripture calls "life in the Spirit."[12] Sadness, heaviness, feelings of despair and hopelessness, and an overall gray outlook on life often stem from a failure to be rightly connected with God.

Frequently, depression masks deeper hurts, such as anger and disappointment with God. Depression is a way of repressing the pain and anger we feel over our lack of intimate relationship with God and others.

One evening Monica gathered with her small group for healing prayer. Gently, the group members began to probe beneath the surface of Monica's life. Monica described long, frenzied days of mind-numbing activities that kept her running until eleven o'clock each night. At first, the group empathized with her busyness. Then, as good friends are supposed to do, they began to explore the function Monica's busyness served in her life.

"I think your schedule works for you, Monica," one friend said. "I think you are running from God. You're afraid of slowing down enough to get to know him."

"You're right," Monica admitted. "Maybe I'm afraid of God."

Several evenings of healing prayer revealed deep wounds in Monica's inner world and a terrifying fear of being rejected by her heavenly

Father. She had developed a lifestyle of frantic activity—Christian activity—so she never had to face her fears of intimacy with God. Monica has recently begun to work on the need for spiritual intimacy in her life. Her depression has not entirely disappeared, but the edge has been taken off. Her healing journey is just beginning. She is learning a lesson many of us must face: lack of spiritual intimacy can make us depressed.

BECOMING RELIGIOUS

Religion is the archrival of intimate spirituality. Follow our Lord across the pages of the Gospels and notice who opposes him. His clashes are not with kings and queens or thieves and bandits, but with the prevailing religious people of the day. Religion, a tiresome system of manmade dos and don'ts, woulds and shoulds—impotent to change human lives but tragically capable of devastating them—is what is left after a true love for God has drained away. Religion is the shell that is left after the real thing has disappeared.

Yahweh was speaking of religion when he thundered, "I cannot bear your evil assemblies. . . . Your appointed feasts my soul hates. They have become a burden to me; I am weary of bearing them."[13]

Jesus was speaking of religion when he said of the spiritual leaders of his day, "They tie up heavy loads and put them on men's shoulders."[14]

Born-again, Bible-believing Christians are not safe from the menace of stale religion. How many of our churches have gone the way of the believers of Laodecia, to whom Christ said, "Because you are lukewarm—neither hot nor cold—I am about to spit you out of my mouth."[15]

When we fail to attach our deepest longings to Christ, religious activity can become a perverse counterfeit of true religion. Hours of sweaty jogging on the church treadmill become a substitute for cultivated intimacy with our divine Friend and Lover. We find ourselves going through the motions of church life. Prayer becomes a quasi-magical means of warding off evil powers instead of a warm dialogue with a Friend. The pastor's sermons no longer hold our attention. We grow numb to the eternal plight of our lost neighbor. Global missions captures little of our heart, money, and prayers. Our heart drifts from the priorities of the kingdom of God. The great stories of the Faith no longer shape our decisions and dreams; lesser tales, tales sprinkled with sensuality and moral darkness—devoid of the heart of God—take their place. Our life quest begins to look remarkably like the life quest of our lost friends and neighbors. This is the all-too-common consequence of failing to build our religious life on the foundation of an intimate connection with Christ.

BURNOUT

A 1991 survey of pastors by the Fuller Institute of Church Growth uncovered the following sober statistics:

> 80% said the ministry had affected their families negatively.
> 75% reported at least one significant stress-related crisis.
> 90% felt inadequately trained to cope with ministry demands.
> 70% said they have a lower self-image now than when they started.
> 70% said they do not have someone they consider a close friend.

Pastors are dropping like RAF planes in the Battle of Berlin. "Our clergy ancestors clung to their saddles for as long as they could sit up and take nourishment," observes church-watcher and futurist Leonard Sweet. "Today we clergy are halfway out the door, retiring posthaste, the spring having gone out of our step. Despite our denial, we know deep inside we are not on top of our ministry; our ministry is on top of us."[16]

A scribbled telephone message appears on my office door. A fellow pastor has collapsed emotionally under the weight of his ministry. Would I please pray for him?

A wide variety of causes sends a pastor tumbling from his horse. Yet there is one common variable in every pastoral postmortem—a loss of intimacy with Christ. Laypeople are just as susceptible to spiritual burnout as pastors. I have witnessed more fallen riders than I care to count.

Debbie, a mother of six and one of our many tireless lay ministers, tumbled into depression after her husband, Gary, had surprised her with a trip to Hawaii a few weeks after her fortieth birthday. With her responsibilities safely taken care of on the other side of the continent and the adrenaline she had been living on drained out, Debbie finally had a chance to stop and take stock of her inner world. She found she did not have much of one left.

"I just crashed," she remembers. "I had been gutting it out, working very hard at a ministry I really didn't enjoy or feel called to." Debbie descended into a black depression and a classic case of pastoral burnout. "I had no joy, no hope. I thought, 'If this is as good as it gets, I want out of here.'"

Debbie and Gary quickly resigned from all their ministry activities as soon as they returned from Hawaii. Days turned into weeks. Debbie pulled away from all but a few friends; the very thought of stepping back into the whirlwind of activity she had lived in before overwhelmed her. Looking back, Debbie wonders how she ever lived the way she once did. "I had everything reversed," she says. "I was doing good things and trying to find Jesus there. God had to teach me that my first concern was my relationship with Jesus."

The instructor God used to teach Debbie this life lesson was Andrew Murray. Many weeks into the dark night of her soul, Debbie took an old copy of Murray's *Abide in Christ* off her shelf and began to read its classic devotions on intimate spirituality. "God used that book to heal me," Debbie remembers thankfully. "I realized I'd been doing so much that I had no time left to abide in Christ."

Those truths have transformed Debbie's life and ministry. "I'm not the same person I used to be," she admits. "I'd never go back to the way I used to be." Now the cornerstone of Debbie's life and ministry is the time she spends each day with Jesus. She says these times reflect her sense of dependency on God. "When I don't get that time," she confesses, "I have little energy for my family or my ministry." What used to be a dull routine has become a life-giving daily rhythm. Debbie reads several Scripture verses and then listens, journaling about whatever she hears God say through his word. "The key is abiding," Debbie believes. These daily times in dialogue with her Lord help her do just that.

Jesus' warning regarding ministering without intimate attachment to him is worth repeating: "If anyone does not remain in me, he is like a branch that is . . . thrown into the fire and burned."[17]

RELATIONAL PROBLEMS

We can only enjoy relational intimacy with other people as we enjoy relational intimacy with Christ. The cherished loved ones in our lives make good friends but poor gods—we dare not ask them to be for us what only God can be. Yet often we do.

Think about a time when a close friend or family member disappointed you. You may have been disappointed because this person truly let you down, perhaps even sinning against you. Possibly your disappointment stems from another reason—perhaps you had gone into the relationship with hidden emotional needs of which neither you nor they were aware.

When we have not bonded with God, when we are not walking daily in a settled sense of our own belovedness, when the voice of Jesus is not the voice that affirms and guides our soul, we inevitably seek that affirmation and guidance somewhere else. Nature abhors a vacuum, and so does our soul. An empty soul will not stay empty for long. When God is not present, a host of lesser gods is always ready to rush in. One of the most common of these pretenders to the throne of our hearts is friendship.

An empty soul will not stay empty for long.

I once heard psychologist Dan Allender warn of the danger of giving people "the power to redeem or destroy you." This power belongs only to God. Yet, when we fail to bond intimately with God, we too quickly yield the right to redeem and destroy to other people—especially significant, strong people who speak powerfully into our lives.

Ann developed intense feelings of bitterness and resentment toward Carol, who had once been a close friend and mentor. Feelings of violent anger rushed forth when Ann had to listen to Carol pray or even speak. Desperate to change, but trapped in her anger, Ann even considered leaving the church—anything to get away from Carol.

Ann shared her struggle with a friend one day over lunch.

"What has Carol done to you?" her friend asked.

Ann thought for a moment. "Really not that much, I guess. I was so excited when she said she wanted to mentor me. At first, it went really well. I learned so much. But . . ."

"But what?"

"Well, our relationship started to change. Carol had another child and I went back to work. We said we'd keep on meeting, but it never worked out. Sometimes I'd leave a message and she wouldn't call back. I'm not sure why that was such a big deal, though. I do the same thing to you now that I am working." Ann smiled at her friend, who smiled and nodded in return.

Ann seemed surprised at how trivial these "crimes" sounded. They certainly did not explain the deep-seated rage that smoldered in her heart toward Carol.

"Do any particular memories stand out?"

Ann's eyes flashed with anger. "Yes," she replied, her entire body tightening. "When Carol promised to disciple me, she said she really loved me and thought I'd be a great leader some day. I remember feeling so loved, so special—feelings I hadn't felt since . . ."

"Since when?"

Ann slowly stirred her tea, deep in thought. Several moments passed.

"Since . . . never," she said softly, running her finger over the rim of her now-empty tea glass. "No one had ever made me feel that way. Not even my own mom."

Ann and her friend met several more times. Ann discovered that she had brought hidden emotional needs into the relationship. She had looked to Carol to be much more than a friend to her. Ann had given Carol too much power in her life. Carol had become, in some ways, like a god to Ann, bestowing Ann with feelings of specialness and worth.

Ann had taken her need for intimacy and nailed it to a friend. And, as inevitably happens, the friend made a poor god. Today Ann still misses the relationship she could have shared with Carol. But the irrational anger is gone. Ann has begun her own quest to know God, knowing all too well the danger of entering into significant relationships with an unbonded soul.[18]

LOSS OF VISION

I recently asked a group of businessmen what their greatest spiritual question was. The runaway answer was, "How do I discover my calling in life?" I believe that God has a special calling for every believer—for dentists, electricians, CEOs, and pastors alike. A calling is God's unique vision for your life. These businessmen were asking one of life's most important questions: How do I discover my life vision?

Vision is birthed out of intimate communion with our Lord. Just as a child is conceived from intimacy between husband and wife, so vision is birthed out of intimacy with God. We discover our calling in life as we come to know the Caller. I find that many people lead vision-less lives because they do not know the One Who Is Vision. They spend their entire lives doing what everyone else thinks they should do, or what needs to be done, or what someone they respect likes to do. They never pause long enough to find out what *Christ* has called them to. When they finish their lives, they are not able to say what Jesus could say as he finished his life: "I have brought you glory on earth by completing the work you have sent me to do." The fact is, they never *knew* what the Father sent them to do.

One reason why I am writing this book is that I have watched too many good men and women trudge through their lives with absolutely no idea of the unique vision God has for them. This is a tragedy—both for themselves and for the people their vision would have touched. Knowing Jesus allows us to know our calling. We will explore how spiritual intimacy births vision in the last chapter of this book.

AN INVITATION TO QUEST TOGETHER

Is it really possible that a relationship with God can be so satisfying that the lesser gods of work or power or sex or drugs or alcohol or relationships or money pale in comparison? Is it really possible to be so "nailed" to God that my self-esteem is rooted in a present experiential awareness of his awesome love for me? Dare I hope that I can bond so tightly to my God that my heart is filled with new vision and my religion becomes a white-hot quest to know and worship the living Christ? Can my relationship with Christ really quench my thirst for love, for approval,

WHEN WE FAIL TO BOND WITH GOD

for a father's applause? Can I truly encounter Christ with such intimacy that I no longer make the pilgrimage to the high places of my addictions? Can Jesus really touch the raw loneliness of my heart? Dare I believe that the hug of Jesus might be as real to me as the hug of a trusted friend? Is this too much to hope for?

No, it is not too much to hope for. In fact, it is the hope of the Gospel. We have been built to connect with God and with other people. Loving God and loving people is the heart of biblical faith. "Love the Lord your God with all your heart and with all your soul and with all your mind. This is the first and greatest commandment," Jesus said. "And the second is like it: 'Love your neighbor as yourself.'"[19] This book is about obeying the first of these commandments: loving God, and being loved by God, with every part of your being.

Loving God and loving people is the heart of biblical faith.

You and I are both on a quest to know God intimately, whether we know it or not. The road we must travel to fulfill this quest is a long and perilous one. The pages that lie before you are written with the prayerful hope that they will encourage you as you walk the often lonely miles of your own pilgrimage.

I have chosen not to write to you as a spiritual guide. I am not far enough along on my own journey to write as a master—as the next chapter sadly demonstrates. My words are written instead as a fellow pilgrim who would like to walk with you along the way. If you are up for some company, take my hand and let's begin.

TWO

MY JOURNEY
BEYOND ADDICTION

The year 1972 was not a good one. America was in turmoil. We were losing our first war. Terrorists turned the Munich Olympics into a war zone. And a hotel called Watergate was about to become a symbol of the dashed hopes of a nation. My struggles, however, had little to do with headlines about troop withdrawals and senate investigations. I had a much bigger problem: surviving Mrs. Alvenia Rhea's sixth grade class.

JACKRABBITS, BEAVERS, AND BUNNIES

Worthingway Elementary School had its own caste system, and it did not take long to figure out how it worked. The better students were whisked away into advanced study groups. Our teachers, sensitive to the emotional trauma caused by such a class system, chose Orwellian code names to disguise the fact that some kids were more on the ball than others. One teacher might divide his class into animals—the bunnies, beavers, and jackrabbits, for example. Another teacher might group her children by colors—"the red reading group will meet in the library today."

No matter what they called us, I was not fooled. If bunnies were the top group, then a bunny I would be. It took me until the sixth grade to claw my way over jackrabbits and beavers into the bunny group. Sixth graders, of course, no longer liked being called "bunnies," so Mrs. Rhea made up another name for the top group, which I cannot remember anymore. But names were not important. I had made it to the top of the elementary school mountain. I had secured a spot in the inner ring. All those years of slogging through Jane, Dick, and Spot had paid off.

The perks of success were everything I had hoped for. Our elite group was left on our own, free to study at our own pace. When Mrs. Rhea needed someone to run an errand to the principal's office, we got the call. I knew too that my parents, both well-educated educators, were pleased by my academic success. Best of all was the delicious sweetness of being a member of the "in" group. We traded knowing glances when a slower student missed a question, and developed our own slang that only insiders could decode, and walked together to Dairy Queen on Friday afternoons for ice cream sundaes.

C. S. Lewis described the phenomenon of the inner ring in an address to the students at King's College in 1944. "You discover gradually, in almost indefinable ways, that it exists and that you are outside it; and then later, perhaps, that you are inside it," he said. "I believe that in all men's lives at certain periods and in many men's lives at all periods . . .one of the most dominant elements is the desire to be inside the local Ring and the terror of being outside." The Oxford moralist then wisely concluded his address with this insight: "This desire is one of the great permanent mainsprings of human action. . . . And unless you take measures to prevent it, this desire is going to be one of the chief motives of your life."[1]

I had never even heard of C. S. Lewis in 1972. But I did know of the alluring power of the inner ring—and of the terror of being left outside it. Already, the desire to achieve, to win favor from my superiors, to outdo everyone else, and to fight my way to the elite group of overachievers had become a driving passion in my life.

Membership Revoked

My membership in the inner ring was revoked shortly before Christmas break. My grades had begun to slip. I lacked the mental discipline to stay focused in an unstructured learning environment. One parent-teacher conference and I was banished once more to the world I had worked so hard to leave—the world of jackrabbits and beavers, the dreaded world of "the average students."

I began to have nightmares. My heart pounding and face wet with sweat, I would sit up in bed and cry out a long, low moan.

"What is it, honey?" my mother would ask, gently shaking me awake.

"It's college," I would stammer. "I dreamed I wasn't accepted into an Ivy League school."

Mom, concerned about my neurosis over academic achievement, took me to see Dr. Park, our family physician. "The boy's getting an ulcer," he told her. "He worries too much." I was worried. So worried that I studied thirty hours for a sixth-grade science exam. So worried that when I lost my 4.0 grade point average—and the chance to be valedictorian—in the last quarter of my junior year, life seemed stripped of purpose. (I had been preparing my graduation speech for five years.) So worried that I secretly discovered who in the college dorm studied the longest, and then made sure I studied one hour more. The nightmares eventually stopped, but my compulsive drive to perform did not.

My parents never pushed me to succeed academically. When the pressure to maintain my 4.0 grade point average began to take a toll on me, they even promised to reward me if I would get a B! I loved Mom and Dad. I respected them. I learned a lesson as I watched them struggle through their own graduate programs and work hard to make their own dreams come true. I learned a lesson when Dad spoke admiringly of his mother Grandma Pat, one of the first women to graduate from Columbia University. I learned a lesson when Mom went back to work to save enough money to send me, in their words, "to any college you can get into." I learned a lesson when the scholarship offers came and the mailbox was filled with letters from people I did not know who said they wanted me to come to their college. I learned a lesson when my name was in the paper for winning a journalism scholarship and when the mothers at the pool whispered, "That young man is going somewhere" when I walked to my life-guarding chair. And I learned a lesson when I returned home from college after my freshman year and found that the girls who just a year before were chasing football players suddenly became interested in dating a guy with a promising career.

Children are smart. They take a look at their world, figure out how to win love and avoid pain, and then work the plan. My plan was well in place long before I encountered Mrs. Rhea's inner ring: Work hard. Achieve much. People will love you. And God will smile.

A SOCIALLY ACCEPTABLE ADDICTION

I did not know at the time that what I was really yearning for was a relationship with God and that my obsessive lust for the holy grail of success was nothing more than a socially acceptable addiction. Years later, I saw myself exposed in the words of psychologist Gerald May.

> After twenty years of listening to the yearnings of people's hearts, I am convinced that all human beings have an inborn desire for God. Whether we are consciously religious or not, this desire is our deepest longing. . . . It gives us meaning. . . . It is a hunger to love, be loved, and to move closer to the Source of love. . . . But something gets in the way. . . . Our desires are captured and we give ourselves over to things that, in our deepest honesty, we really do not want. . . . Addiction . . . turns us away from love. . . . Addiction attaches desire, bonds and enslaves the energy of desire to certain specific behaviors, things, or people. . . . Addiction is the most powerful psychic enemy of humanity's desire for God.[2]

My conversion to Christianity removed the guilt of sin from my life but not the obsessive drive to achieve. The ministry became another way to keep score. I became the leader of the Fellowship of Christian Athletes and my high school youth group, and I began Bible studies in my dorm during my freshman year at college. I climbed the ranks of Campus Crusade for Christ, doing whatever it took to win the applause of my leaders and earn a spot in Crusade's inner ring. I graduated from Northwestern on a sweltering June Sunday in 1983 with a degree in journalism in my hand and a firm belief in my heart that if I worked hard enough I could do anything I wanted to in life. "There are two kinds of people in the world," I remember telling a friend. "Some people run the world. Others just watch. I'm in the first group."

The belief system of my addiction was now firmly established.

"Work hard and do well in the ministry and people will love you."
"Work hard and do well in the ministry and God will love you."

Alongside these core convictions were some darker companions.

"Fail in the ministry and you are unlovable."
"God loves you only when you perform well for him."

Even deeper hid another longing, one that would not surface consciously for a dozen more years. It was a longing to find father figures and please them. Once I no longer lived at home, I turned to other mature men to father me.

Campus Crusade excels in discipling their students, and I was discipled by some great men. I gave them power in my life—too much power, I would later learn—and found life in their words of encouragement and praise. I had found a life strategy that worked, or so it seemed. Find a ministry, work hard, do better than most of your peers, and drink in the praise of the father figures of the movement.

A year later I was enrolled in seminary.

FEEDING MY ADDICTION AT TALBOT

Addicts have an uncanny ability to find their fix no matter where life takes them. Drug addicts can score a hit in Paris as easily as in Peoria, and sex addicts can find a prostitute in Boston as easily as in Budapest. C. S. Lewis, in his remarks at King's College, gently chided his audience. "And here, too, at your university—shall I be wrong in assuming that at this very moment, invisible to me, there are several rings[3] . . . present in this room?"[4] The Talbot School of Theology became the perfect place for me to feed my addiction. I quickly found the way into Talbot's inner ring.

I took more classes than most, preached on the weekends, served on the staff of my church, taught two courses of freshman English, and still made high marks. Men my father's age taught our classes—godly, kind men who rewarded earnest young students with good grades and preaching opportunities. My middle year I won the Louis Talbot award as the student most exemplifying the values of our seminary. My senior year I won the homiletics award for the senior with the best preaching skills. My hard work won me something much more significant—the respect of several father figures who began to mentor me.

The mentoring relationship that would eventually have the most impact on my life was with Jack Tarr, a physician and fellow student at Talbot. Jack, twelve years older than I, represented everything I wanted to be as a Christian man. He was head over heels in love with his wife Kathy, a patient father to four children, and so committed to ministry that he had put his medical career on hold to study in seminary.

We began to spend time together and soon found we shared a common vision for ministry. Jack, Kathy, my wife Sandi, and I began to discuss planting a church together. In July of 1987, we moved to Knoxville, Tennessee to join the Tarrs in planting Fellowship Church. We held our first meeting in the Tarr's basement in July. Twenty people attended. The future looked bright. Those core beliefs I had learned in elementary school were proving to be true again: Work hard, minister well, and people will love you. God will smile. And the fathers will applaud.

The Problem of Getting What You Ask For

The next several years gave me no reason to doubt the success formula that had worked so well for me the first twenty-five years of my life. I took two part-time jobs and began the church with the rest of my time. We started services in the fall and doubled our attendance, then moved to a junior high school cafeteria, and quickly tripled in size. Seven years later we moved into our new building and attendance rose from nine hundred to two thousand.

The trappings of evangelical success soon began to come my way— we were honored as one of America's fastest growing churches and cited in church growth books. Articles on our church's ministries appeared frequently in our denominational magazine. When the presidency of our denomination became open, I was invited to apply. Attendance continued to rise. I began to receive numerous requests to speak from around the country and overseas. Many of the life goals I had set when I was in college were being fulfilled. I completed a doctorate and published my first book. Sandi and I presided over a home filled with the laughter of four wonderful, healthy children. We built another, much larger, worship center to accommodate the swelling crowds, and planted our first daughter church. As my thirties drew to a close, it appeared I could say with David, "The boundary lines have fallen for me in pleasant places; surely I have a delightful inheritance."[5]

Appearances, however, are deceiving. What I had inherited as my ministry continued to expand was anything but delightful. I had inherited a broken inner world. Even as my pastoral "career" was scoring high marks, my inner world was slowly unraveling.

HAUNTED BY PAUL

The first hint that all was not well came when I was preaching through Romans chapters five through eight. Paul's descriptions of our relationship with Christ began to haunt me. He speaks of a God who "poured out his love into our hearts by the Holy Spirit" and of being "united with Christ." He claims that "those who are led by the Spirit of God are sons of God" and speaks of a relationship with Christ so intimate that "the Spirit himself intercedes for us with groans that words cannot express."[6]

> The horror of addiction is that we allow God-substitutes to fill our souls. And we lose our desire for the real thing.

I knew little of an intimate friendship with Christ so personal that his love poured like a waterfall over my heart, so personal that I could say my life was actually "led by the Spirit of God." As a card-carrying evangelical, I often spoke of a personal relationship with Christ. Yet it had not occurred to me that this relationship might be so personal that Christ, Christ alone, might touch my throbbing heart-cry for someone to say, "Well done."

My degrees, my reputation as a promising young pastor, the affirmation of the fathers in my life had satisfied the need for affirmation. The horror of addiction is that we allow

God-substitutes to fill our souls. And we lose our desire for the real thing. "Spiritually, addiction is a deep-seated form of idolatry," writes Gerald May. "Addiction uses up desire."[7]

ON TEARING DOWN HIGH PLACES

I did not return to these truths from Romans until the lesser gods of success and applause began to fail me. Could my relationship with Christ be so satisfying that lesser gods would lose their attractiveness? Is it possible to nurture a relationship with Christ so real that the pseudo-gods I had run after for so long would no longer seduce me? If so, how? How do I create that kind of relationship? I know the rules of obtaining the false intimacy of the inner ring. What are the rules of true intimacy? I was asking the right questions. I wish I had been wise enough to ask them long before.

"Repent!" God told Israel through the prophet Ezekiel. "Turn from your idols."[8] God viewed the idols his people had turned to as false lovers. He wept, a wounded Lover, as his beloved people "engaged in prostitution with . . . your lustful neighbors."[9] When renewal broke out among the people of God, it typically began with the tearing down of false idols. King Hezekiah sparked revival when he "did what was right in the eyes of the LORD" and "removed the high places" where his people worshiped false gods.[10]

Personal renewal also begins with the tearing down of idols, the exposure of our addictions. When we are so blinded by our addictions that we cannot see the bars of our own prison, God, in his thunderous grace, often intervenes on our behalf, destroying the high places in our lives and calling us back to our first Love. He began intervening that way in my life on a blustery, gray November Monday with a telephone call I will never forget.

LESSONS FROM A CHILDREN'S CANCER WARD

The call came from Children's Hospital. My then seven-year-old daughter had been suffering from a prolonged case of mono, and Sandi had taken her in for a routine ultrasound. It had not occurred to me that something else could be wrong. The ultrasound discovered that Bryden had a three-pound cancerous tumor hiding behind her kidney. Within hours, we were meeting with the pediatric oncologist and learning more than we ever wanted to know about the side effects of chemotherapy on a child's body. I still had wood chips on my paint-stained college letterman's jacket when we walked out of the hospital that night, vaguely aware that a strange new chapter had just opened in our lives.

Every Monday for the next eighteen months we took Bryden to the children's oncology unit for her chemotherapy treatments. We watched her hair fall out, caressed her forehead when she vomited after each treatment, and prayed silently during each blood transfusion that no soiled blood had contaminated the supply. We became friends with the wonderful staff of the children's oncology clinic and the precious families that suffer there. We celebrated for the children who left the clinic cancer-free and wept for those who would never leave at all. Each year, the survivors attend a weeklong summer camp. The camp ends with a ceremony in a special garden dedicated to the children who could not return.

For the first time in my life, succeeding was not my top priority. Surviving was. Nearly four years have passed since I first saw the blurry oval on the ultrasound that threatened to take my daughter's life. Remarkably, I look back on those times with both pain and fondness, for it was the first time in my life I felt totally loved without performing. At Children's Hospital, I was not a pastor or an author or a speaker, but a father with a broken heart. That was all I had to be. Our church and family wrapped us in love, and prayers from around the world upheld us.

Sometimes during our stays at Children's I wandered downstairs to a small multi-faith chapel. God's love encountered me there in a way I had never experienced before—the love of a Father for a hurting son, a love "poured out" into my heart such as Paul described to the Romans. The Father affirmed the Son as his beloved one *before* Jesus ever did anything for him. Finally I knew what that kind of love felt like. And I wanted more.

The experience of God's love during that season was mingled with deep pain. As the months wore on, I slipped in and out of depression, and often lost a battle with fear. Confusion stalked me, especially at the end of long days in the hospital. My airtight theology forbade my mind from asking the unanswerable questions suffering parents have hurled at heaven for thousands of years—but my heart asked them anyway. *Why my daughter? Did I not pray for her more than most parents? Would we win this battle? Would we be able to go on if we lost it?*

Unknown to me at the time, the divine Surgeon was cutting deeply into my soul, penetrating the addictive belief system I had spent thirty-four years putting into place— a system rooted in the lie that hard work and faithful service protect you from pain. A deadly illness had attacked my soul, and I was not able to heal myself from it. God's violent grace tore into me and ripped apart my self-built strength. Still, I clung to a strand of my own power. It would take several more relapses before I would lie completely helpless and desperate for God's healing touch.

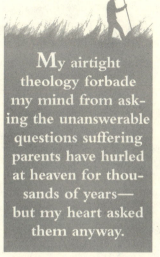

My airtight theology forbade my mind from asking the unanswerable questions suffering parents have hurled at heaven for thousands of years— but my heart asked them anyway.

The Prison of Success

One of the ironies of tragedy is that life goes on without you. Our church continued to grow, and with it, my responsibilities. But something was different now. The fire and energy that marked my first years in ministry had ebbed. The explosive growth that earned us the reputation as "one of America's fastest growing churches" had become a ball and chain. We were not able to keep pace with our growth, and people were falling through the cracks. Many of them left the church, some of them angry and disappointed. Some of the "father figures" I had looked to early on said goodbye as well, taking a piece of my heart with them. A fund-raising campaign for our new worship center fell far short of our goal. Some questioned my motives in wanting a new building. Was I just interested in building my own kingdom?

"What about the poor?" a good friend shouted at me in a leader's meeting one night. "How can you build a five million dollar building when people are sleeping on the streets in our town every night?"

Ministry became an endless series of meetings and long days filled with solving problems that never seemed to go away. I lost my joy—and again slipped into mild depression. For the first time, I found myself considering leaving the ministry. My love for the people slowly became stained by bitterness, and I often complained to my inner circle about their "lack of submission to authority." Critical letters sometimes brought me to tears. I was becoming an angry, tired man. The myths that had guided my life were eroding under the weight of life.

> Work hard.
> Minister well.
> People will love you.
> God will smile.
> And the fathers will applaud.

I had worked hard. I had tried to minister well. But the people were mad. God was not smiling. And the fathers no longer clapped.

A PAINFUL FAILURE

Anyone familiar with the dynamics of healthy relationships probably realizes that my hunger for father figures set my relationship with Jack up for failure from the beginning. I can empathize with good Christian people who find themselves on the brink of divorce and wondering how they got there. Jack and I almost divorced—and nearly broke our church apart in the process.

The Tarrs and the Banisters struggled relationally from the earliest days of our church, even though we loved one another deeply. Neither couple ever intentionally wanted to hurt the other. Well aware that relational problems among leaders are the death rattle of the church, we worked hard at our friendship, devoting entire weekends to working through our differences. Yet somehow we continued to hurt each other. Seasons of separation from each other (made easier by a rapidly growing church) were interrupted by intense attempts at reconciliation—none of which seemed to "stick."

During the winter of 1998 our elders became convicted that our body was suffering relationally. We became convinced that corporate sin had entered the camp and that God's blessing was being withheld from us because we had not put relational sin away through repentance and reconciliation. Jack and I committed to another attempt to heal the wounds in our relationship.

Our first meetings succeeded only in opening old wounds and causing them to bleed freely again. We asked the elders to get involved. What followed over the next sixth months was the most painful season of both of our lives. Jack and I met, first alone and then with our wives, and submitted to an intense reconciliation process that took months to complete.

God touched our relationship and gave us the breakthrough the four of us had desperately needed. Today, Jack and I minister side-by-side in our church with renewed love for one another. We are living proof that irreconcilable differences can be reconciled and that no relationship is worthy of giving up on. Thank you, Jesus!

Healing begun is not healing finished, and God led our church into a season of Solemn Assembly.[11] Night after night we worked through relational reconciliation, first among our elders, then among our elders and staff, then with estranged groups in the church. We shut down most of the ministries in our church and asked people not to start new ones. Our courageous church family took this season very seriously. Engaged couples delayed their wedding plans. Businessmen waited to make major decisions. It was a sober season of reflection and repentance.

I preached a series of ten messages on corporate sin and repentance and asked the people to pray for God's conviction regarding sin in our church. We asked Jesus to "write us a letter," similar to the letters written to the seven churches in Revelation 2 and 3. On Friday night, October 16, we gathered as a people for a Solemn Assembly, read "the letter" from Jesus to us as a people, and spent four hours confessing our sins and covenanting to keep God's relational standards as a people. God keeps his promises. He heard our confession that night, and the blessing of his manifest presence is gradually returning to our worship services and ministries.

The Solemn Assembly broke me. Some of my brokenness was the "godly sorrow[that brings repentance]"[12] as I bore the burden of my relational sin and its impact on our body. One Sunday morning after a sermon I broke down in the pulpit and sobbed for ten minutes, mourning the relational poison that had seeped into our body under my watch. I now realize I was also mourning the death of my addiction to success. I had led a church that did not love well. The promising young man had failed.

A good bit of my pain during the Solemn Assembly, though, was not from God. Our Father promises to hurl our sin into the deepest ocean, and he faithfully kept that promise. Our body began to heal. But I remained stuck, unable to appropriate God's grace for myself. The Accuser of the Brethren attempted to impale me on the fragments of my old belief system, and almost succeeded. I led the Solemn Assembly that Friday night, and as I confessed our corporate sins I also felt I was confessing my complete failure as a leader and a pastor. The myths I had lived by no longer worked. The idol I had fashioned with my own hands now lay heedless at my feet. I had sacrificed everything to get people to love me. I had tried my hardest to make God smile. I had done everything I could to hear the fathers clap. And I had failed. I could feel myself spiraling once again into exhaustion and depression.

Life stops for no one, and Tuesday morning I was back to work, meeting with my colleagues to determine how best to squeeze out the poison that had invaded the body.

And nothing worked.

THE FINAL BLOW

When you have been in the ministry for a while you become sensitive to the times in your life when you are ministering apart from God's blessing and power. I was in one of those times. Everything I touched turned to ashes. Every decision I made left a relational wake behind me. I crushed several dear friends and faithful coworkers. No matter what I did, we could not move forward.

Finally, in March, a friend and fellow elder came to my office. "Can I read you a letter I wrote you?" he asked.

"Yes," I said, wondering what was in it.

My friend's letter was the medicine that penetrated straight to my illness—and knocked me flat. He questioned my ability to provide organizational leadership for the church and wondered if it was time for me to take a different role. I was crushed. Yet at the same time, I had to admit that I was wondering the same thing. The next Saturday night I was alone in the church working on the next day's sermon. I could not concentrate; I felt the Spirit calling me to do business with him. I quietly walked into the nearly finished worship center, knelt on the fresh carpet, and placed my church keys on the altar.

"Jesus," I prayed. "I simply do not have what it takes to lead this church. Something has to change. I keep hurting people. I did not go into the ministry to hurt people. It kills me to hurt people I love. It just is not working. Something has to give. If you can still use me around here, I would love that. But if not, I understand. This season of ministry is over." I went to my computer and wrote the elders a letter, telling them that I found truth in my friend's letter and wanted to explore other ways to lead the church.

The elders graciously received my letter and, over the next several months, shaped a role for me better suited to my teaching and writing gifts. Others more gifted than I now run the church on a daily basis, and Jack does an excellent job as the chairman of the elder board. The breezes of renewal are blowing again. Joy is returning in my life, as is my passion for ministry. Our church is probably healthier now than it has been since its inception.

I had lunch recently with a wise friend and fellow author and shared my concerns about this book with him. "I'm not sure I'm far enough along to write this," I told him in between bites of blackened-chicken salad. "I'm still healing, still learning how to live in a new way."

"You don't have to solve everything," he smiled. "Just tell your story. Life doesn't usually play out as a nice before and after picture, does it?"

I took his advice. I hope you do not mind an author who has not figured everything out. I have not got many answers. But I am learning what the questions are. Here's the Big One everyone who quests well must eventually ask: *Is Jesus enough?*

Every addict must answer this question. And by the way, we are all addicts. Every one of us is born with a bent toward making our life work apart from God. Every one of us figures out ways to avoid pain on our own. This is the essence of original sin—being born with a twisted soul that would rather feed an addiction than worship the Creator. "To be alive is to be addicted,"[13] observes Gerald May. Conversion, then, is turning from our addictions to an intimate, soul-satisfying relationship with Jesus Christ. Sanctification is the lifelong journey of deepening that relationship and renouncing lesser lovers.

Putting the Map Back Together Again

A friendship with Jesus can satisfy the deepest longings of our hearts *if* we know how to nurture that friendship. I turned to both familiar and unfamiliar places to find help in rebuilding this friendship. I am an evangelical by heritage. My journey toward the embrace of Christ has led me to dust off some classic evangelical teaching about the art of spiritual friendship with Christ. I cannot wait to share with you what I learned as I sat at the feet of evangelicalism's wisest writers and teachers on the spiritual life.

> **A** friendship with Jesus can satisfy the deepest longings of our hearts *if* we know how to nurture that friendship.

My journey beyond addiction into the arms of Jesus has also encouraged me to drink deeply from the waters of the charismatic renewal. I must admit that I had evangelical apprehensions about bathing in the streams running through my charismatic cousins' property. But drowning men are not picky about who throws them a lifejacket. My hunger to know Jesus with *all* my heart and *all* my mind and *all* my soul drove me toward my charismatic brothers and sisters in pursuit of their wisdom on becoming better friends with Jesus. I am just as excited to share with you what I gleaned from the best and brightest of the charismatic movement.

I have discovered that these two strands of spirituality complement each other beautifully. These two spiritual traditions reveal different mysteries of God's heart. It is as if each tradition has been given part of the remedy to find healing and wholeness in Christ. Separately, the traditions provide only partial health. Bring the two pieces together, and a clearer diagnosis emerges.

The purpose of this book is to bring the two halves together. My prayer for you, my friend, is that the story of this wounded healer might intersect with your story, and together we might know Christ so intimately that the lesser gods of our addictions never again draw our affections away from the One Who Eternally Satisfies.

How do we build an intimate friendship with a Person we cannot see? Thankfully, God has provided us with a model to use as a pattern for our relationship with Christ. This model is marriage.

THREE

AS CHRIST LOVED
THE CHURCH

I got married wearing tube socks. White ones. We were running late and I had lost the dress socks we rented from the tuxedo place; it was going to be either bare skin or Kmart white sticking out when we knelt for prayer. I went with white.

Socks were the last thing on my mind when we finally pulled out of Sandi's parents' house in our '78 beige Pinto with a peeling vinyl roof.

We boarded the plane for Hawaii early the next morning and began one of the best weeks of our lives. I cannot imagine a more romantic honeymoon spot than the Hawaiian Islands. We rode mopeds along the shores of Oahu, watched surfers on the Bonzai pipeline, snorkeled in the same bay Elvis swam in, took a moonlight cruise, and kissed a whole lot.

And then we came home.

A cold snap had hit LA, and our frostbitten Pinto refused to leave her stall. Shivering and loaded down with luggage, leis, and pineapples, we waved down a car and got a jump. The parking attendants at the Los Angeles airport do not care if you are honeymooners or FBI agents—everybody pays. I forked over half a week's salary to pay for our parking and we headed up the 5 Freeway to Anaheim where our little love nest awaited us. (We soon found out that our apartment had a special bonus attraction—Disneyland fireworks every night at nine. And I do mean *every* night.)

Our first year was difficult. Sandi had a challenging job as a claims adjuster for Travelers Insurance and I became a youth pastor in a town forty-five minutes away. I had spent a lot more time thinking about the wedding night than the actual marriage—and it showed.

I knew I was in over my head when we had our first fight as a married couple. I do not remember what we fought about; I do remember that Sandi was in tears. Terrified of a woman crying and frantic to put a stop to it as quickly as I could, I brought out a piece of notebook paper and said, "Honey, just write down what's bothering you and we'll solve this right now." Sandi failed to appreciate my kind, sensitive style of treating her like a differential equation—and the night went downhill from there.

We have now passed the fifteenth wedding anniversary mark and are well on our way to our twentieth. With God's help we have built a good marriage. It has not been easy. We have visited counselors, asked for help from friends, attended conferences, confessed our sins, cried a little, laughed a lot, held each other outside the surgery door on the sixth floor of Children's Hospital, endured Lamaze birth classes (I learned to say, "Get the epidural!"), been mad at each other, said we were sorry, sat through a zillion swim meets and dance recitals, and done our best to weave our lives into one common dance before God.

The Picture of Marriage

A little boy once woke up during a violent thunderstorm and began to cry. His father told the boy to pray and ask God to help him not be afraid. "But I want a God with skin on," the boy sobbed. The example of marriage "puts skin on" our relationship with Jesus.

Scripture often describes the believer's relationship with Christ as a marriage union. In the Old Testament, God frequently dons the imagery of the Groom and relates to Israel as his beloved bride.[2] The New Testament also encourages us to use the language of the bride and Groom to describe our intimate relationship with Christ. The great anthem of praise in Revelation 19:7 declares, "Let us rejoice and be glad and give him glory! For the wedding of the Lamb has come, and his bride has made herself ready."

Paul centers his doctrine of Christian marriage in the same imagery:

> Wives, submit to your husbands as to the Lord. For the husband
> is the head of the wife as Christ is the head of the church, his

body, of which he is the Savior. Now as the church submits to Christ, so also wives should submit to their husbands in everything. Husbands, love your wives, just as Christ loved the church and gave himself up for her to make her holy, cleansing her by the washing with water through the word, and to present her to himself as a radiant church, without stain or wrinkle or any other blemish, but holy and blameless. In the same way, husbands ought to love their wives as their own bodies. He who loves his wife loves himself. After all, no one ever hated his own body, but he feeds and cares for it, just as Christ does the church—for we are members of his body. "For this reason a man will leave his father and mother and be united to his wife, and the two will become one flesh." This is a profound mystery—but I am talking about Christ and the church. However, each one of you also must love his own wife as he loves himself, and the wife must respect her husband.[3]

Many of the couples I marry ask me to share the Gospel as a part of the wedding ceremony. Initially, I wove the Gospel message into the end of my wedding homily. Then a friend pointed out that the symbolism of the bride and the groom preparing to wed *is* the Gospel! Now I pause at the beginning of the service and say, "The Bible compares Christ's love for us with a groom's love for his bride. Just as Mark pursued Terry and asked her to join him in a lifelong covenant of marriage, so Christ pursues each of you and invites you to join him for all eternity. Terry had to respond to Mark's invitation to begin their covenant relationship together. In the same way, we must respond to Christ's invitation by turning from our sins and submitting to him as our Savior and Lord."

This is the mystery: the one-flesh union between husband and wife in marriage is a picture of our union with Jesus Christ.

HOW CAN A MAN BE A BRIDE?

The first time I began to think about this metaphor in Scripture, I balked. I want to be a lot of things in life—and a bride is not one of them. How can a man relate to this biblical metaphor?

Elisabeth Elliot helps us get started answering this question by reminding us that "the essence of masculinity is initiation and the essence of femininity is response."

God loves us first. God initiates salvation by sending his Son to die for us. We respond to his love. We receive the gift of salvation. We respond to his gracious offer of eternal life. C. S. Lewis states, "What is above and beyond all things is so masculine that we are all feminine in relation to it."[5] Men, the bride and groom metaphor does not intend to emasculate us. God is not asking us to become women. He is asking us to acknowledge that in our relationship with him, he initiates and we respond.

> God is asking us to acknowledge that in our relationship with him, he initiates and we respond.

The marriage metaphor will be a helpful guide to us in the chapters ahead. Let's linger a little longer over this metaphor before we press ahead. What is God trying to say to us?

YODA THEOLOGY

My family enjoys Star Wars. We recently became the proud owners of genuine battery-operated light sabers, just like the kind Luke and Darth duel with in the end of *The Empire Strikes Back*. After dinner we occasionally clear out the family room and duel to the death, or at least until bath time. I like to talk to the kids about the spiritual themes in the films. We have talked about what it means to stand up against evil, how not to yield to temptation, and whether or not Wookies go to heaven.

Star Wars, of course, is not just a fast-paced science fiction tale. George Lucas has written a deeply spiritual myth that puts into memorable lines principles from eastern religion that are often difficult for Westerners to understand. The spiritual sage of Star Wars is a tiny little, green fellow with bad skin and big ears named Yoda. The theology of Star Wars is woven throughout the film, but it is spelled out in detail in a discussion Yoda has with his protégé Luke, whom he is training to be a Jedi knight. Luke is unable to lift his ship from the swamp. Yoda explains that the reason is his failure to understand the force. "My ally is the force and a powerful ally it is,"Yoda begins. "Life creates it, makes it grow. Its energy surrounds and binds us." Then, "You must feel the force. Here. Between you, me, the tree, the rock, everywhere. Yes, even between the land and the ship."

We can learn some good lessons about bravery and honor and courage from movies like Star Wars. What we cannot learn from Star Wars, though, is what the God of the Bible is like. Because the God of the Bible is not a force. He is a person.

Our relationship with Jesus differs significantly from Luke's relationship with the force. A marriage involves a loving, mutual relationship between two living people. We must start out on our quest for intimacy with Christ understanding that we are pursuing a person, not a force. Jesus was and still is a person, just like you. He has feelings. He makes plans. He desires relationship. He can be disappointed, grieved, and sad. The relationship we seek is a personal relationship. Jesus said so himself. He told his disciples, "I no longer call you servants. . . . I have called you friends."[6]

"Christianity," notes Leslie Weatherhead in his book *The Transforming Friendship*, "is the acceptance of the gift of the friendship of Jesus."[7]

BEYOND FRIENDSHIP

Marriage is the richest of all human friendships because marriage partners unite in soul, life, and body. A married couple enjoys an intimacy no two other people can possibly share. Our hearts crave this union:

> Deep body-and-soul intimacy with another person is rare. We all desire it. We yearn for someone to know us and then desire to know even more. We long for someone to know us beyond the perceptible to the depths of what even we do not comprehend. We want a person with whom we can be "naked," a person who will not judge us and who will find in our presence an unreserved delight.[8]

Significantly, this powerful description of marital union makes an excellent description of what we hope to taste in Christ. Our relationship with him presses beyond friendship and moves into a real, spiritual union. "Marriage is the closest bond that is possible between two human beings," writes Mike Mason. "As it was originally designed, marriage was a union to end all unions, the very last word, and the first, in human intimacy. . . . There is just no other means of getting closer to another human being."[9] So, too, with Christ. We are more than passing acquaintances or even good buddies. We are *married* to him—spiritually united in a way that transcends any other relationship.

I recently spent an evening helping a friend move. The home he was moving into had gone on the market because the couple that owned it was divorcing. When we arrived at the new home to unload, the garage was still filled with the possessions of a disintegrating family. Notes written with magic marker on 3 X 5 index cards explained which pile belonged to the wife and which pile belonged to the husband. "Cleaner for Mike's car" one said. A lone sand pail rusted in the backyard. No note explained where it was supposed to end up. It began to rain. I felt very sad, as if I were witnessing a funeral. Except this time a family was in the casket.

Something glorious is crushed when a marriage dies. A union intended until death is unmercifully severed. The tremendous destructive power of divorce illustrates the unique power of the marriage union. We are to think of this kind of union when we consider what it means to be in relationship with Christ.

"He who unites himself with the Lord," wrote Paul, "is one with him in spirit."[10]

No other religion makes such an astounding claim. Buddhists do not claim to *know* the Buddha nor do Muslims hope to *know* Mohammed. "Members of other faiths look back to the founder they revere," remarks John Stott. "But to us Jesus is more than a teacher of the ancient past. He is our living Lord and Savior, whom we know in the closeness of a vital and loving relationship."[11]

But what does this really mean?

Our understanding of union with Christ depends greatly on our worldview. Western believers tend to see the spiritual world as living in a different plane than the material world. We see God as "up there" and ourselves as "down here." The spiritual world and the physical world are separate in our minds. We do not expect these two worlds to interact much. When God does "break through" into our daily lives, we call it a "miracle." Miracles, by definition, are events that are not normal. Normal is life "down here."

N̲o other religion makes such an astounding claim. Buddhists do not claim to *know* the Buddha nor do Muslims hope to *know* Mohammed.

Each of us interprets Scripture through the lens of our worldview. What happens when I read about my union with Christ through the lens of a Western worldview? I must interpret Paul's teaching symbolically. My union with Christ, then, is not a real union. Christ, after all, is "up there." I cannot expect to commune with him in any personal, tangible way. Christ can easily become "some vague and distant figure—an absentee landlord who used to do wonderful things and who someday may do them again."[12] Union with Christ, then, is like a soldier's loyalty to a general he has never met.

Nonwestern cultures, however, see the world much differently. These cultures see the spiritual world and the physical world as overlapping. The kingdom of heaven is intermingled with the kingdom of earth. God, or the gods, are not "up there" but "right here."

Many have pointed out that while no worldview is perfect, this supernatural worldview of third world cultures is much more biblical than our present Western one. Jesus went to great lengths in his teaching to argue for a "blended" worldview where the spiritual world fully merged with the physical world. "The kingdom of God has come upon you,"[13] Jesus declared after casting out a demon. "The kingdom of God is near you,"[14] he instructed his disciples to say on their first training journey.

Seen through this lens, our union with Christ is far more than mere symbolism—it is a relationship between two real people made possible as the Spirit of Christ literally fills us. An actual transaction takes place. Divine spirit and human spirit mingle together in my own physical body. I am possessed by the spirit of God. I can say with Paul, "I no longer live, but Christ lives in me."[15]

Sandi and I dated long distance for two years before we married. She was finishing up school in Los Angeles while I was completing my studies in Chicago. We kept our relationship alive primarily by letter. I loved to receive Sandi's letters, and often read and reread them in my fraternity room. Yet how I longed for the day we would be married and could share more than pen and ink! Those two years of waiting were, I think, the longest two years of my life. Our love for one another was real and growing as we related to one another across the gulf of space and time, but it was incomplete.

For many in the West, relationship with Christ is like my long-distance, letter-writing romance. Our love for Christ is real, but reading his letters is as close as we are going to get to really knowing him. When we put on the glasses of a supernatural, biblical worldview, everything changes. We realize that Christ is in our midst. We really can be married and share life together. The days of long-distance dating are gone.

ANSWERING THE QUESTIONS OF INTIMACY

On the night of my wedding day, Dad was driving me back to Sandi's house so we could pick up clothes before leaving on the honeymoon. "Well, the hard part is over," I said, referring to the seemingly endless wedding plans that had now been fulfilled.

"The hard part's just beginning," Dad said. He was right.

Great marriages are created, not decreed. Surviving a wedding ceremony is no guarantee of an enduring, satisfying, intimate marriage relationship. What you do *after* the ceremony determines the future of your relationship.

Couples who have built intimate, passionate marriages have successfully answered four crucial questions about their relationship. These are the same questions we must answer as we deepen our relationship with Christ.

How Do I Hear Jesus' Voice?

Not long after we returned from our Hawaiian honeymoon, I realized that Sandi and I were not communicating very well. We seemed to be speaking different languages. She would try to share her heart with me, but I would be on an entirely different channel.

Marriages do not move toward intimacy without each partner knowing how to hear what the other partner is really trying to say. The same is true in our relationship with Jesus. We must learn how to hear his voice. We must discern what is really on his heart.

Evangelicals teach us that Jesus speaks to us through his Word. Charismatics agree and remind us that we can hear Jesus' voice through the prophetic gifts as well. How do I hear the voice of Jesus? We will see how these two traditions wrestle with this question in chapters 4 and 5.

How Do I Share My Heart with Jesus?

This question is just as important as the first one. Lovers must learn not only how to listen, they must also learn how to speak in a way that can be understood. When I married Sandi, I had just completed a bachelor's degree in journalism. I had spent four years and a lot of my parents' hard-earned money learning how to communicate. Somehow those skills failed me when it came to really sharing my heart with Sandi. Interpersonal communication, I found, was much harder than writing a newspaper story. Sharing my heart was an entirely different type of communication than sharing facts.

We need to grapple with this same question as we consider knowing Jesus. How do we share our hearts with him? How can we communicate with him in a way that is satisfying to both of us? Evangelical spirituality teaches us that prayer is how we share our hearts with Jesus. Charismatic spirituality tells us that praying in a spiritual language is also helpful in expressing our heart's deepest needs. We will explore both these answers in chapters 6 and 7.

How Do I Handle Disappointment with Jesus?

Disappointment is inevitable in a marriage. We sin. We fail. We let one another down. One of the make-or-break questions that determines the future of any marriage is: What will I do when my lover disappoints me?

Strange as it may sound, disappointment is a factor in our relationship with Christ as well. He does not sin, fail, or let us down. Yet we can become disappointed with him when the shadows of a fallen world fall upon our life. Author Philip Yancey wrote an entire book called *Disappointment with God*. Painfully, the dedication reads, "For my brother, who is still disappointed." Yancey says in his opening words that he has interviewed many people who are disappointed with God. "I found that for many people there is a large gap between what they expect from their Christian faith and what they actually experience," he writes. What do we do when we are disappointed with God?

How should a believer confront the suffering that cannot be escaped on this earth? How can pain drive us toward Christ instead of away from him? Evangelicals emphasize that some of our richest encounters with God can take place in the midst of suffering. Charismatics stress that God still heals today, and that he still responds to the cries of his people to deliver them from their pains. These times of rescue, healing, and deliverance can be times of great intimacy with a compassionate God. Chapters 8 and 9 show how both suffering and healing can lead us into deeper intimacy with Christ.

How Can I Stay Faithful to Jesus?

Marriage vows are not easy to keep. All the powers of hell conspire to make us break them.

"He was unfaithful."

How many times have we agonized over hearing those painful words?

Spiritual faithfulness is equally difficult. How do we stay true to the One we love? How can we avoid the spiritual adultery that so often characterized Israel? How can we escape the spiritual traps that so often threaten our passion for Christ so we can say with Paul at the end of our life, "I have fought the good fight, I have finished the race, I have kept the faith"?[17]

Evangelical teachers and writers call us to a disciplined life. Good marriages take hard work and wise choices, resisting the

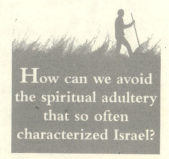

How can we avoid the spiritual adultery that so often characterized Israel?

flesh and obedience to what we know is right. The same is true if we are to kindle a lifelong romance with Christ. Charismatic teachers and writers would not disagree, even though their literature more frequently encourages the reader with the hope of "special moments" with the Savior—divine breakthroughs where God crashes into our lives and we make a giant leap forward in our spiritual progress. Like a great weekend getaway with your spouse, these divine interventions are critical to maintaining "a long obedience in the same direction."[18]

Chapters 10 and 11 are devoted to helping us finish our quests well.

FOUR

HEARING THE VOICE
OF A DANCING FATHER

Y ou didn't hear me." Sandi's eyes turned away and our conversation ended. I had heard her words, but not her heart. And it hurt her.

The first task in building an intimate marriage is learning to hear one another. Intimacy is relational closeness, and relational closeness requires mutual understanding—really knowing in your heart of hearts what the person you love is saying.

I have been trained to be a pretty good listener. I know how to keep eye contact and have been trained in the therapeutic technique called "active listening." I am fairly sensitive to my body language when Sandi speaks, trying to keep my posture as open and receptive as possible to her. And yet often, painfully often, I miss those important words that she is saying. I listen, but do not hear. And an opportunity for intimacy is stolen.

Sometimes, though, I do hear. These times of true listening are the most intimate moments in our marriage. When Sandi's heart connects with my heart and God gives me the grace to gently draw out the deep waters that flow through her inner world, a bond forms between us that is intense and passionate. Nothing is more intimate, more romantic, more affirming than listening well and truly hearing the words of her heart.

THE HEART OF EVANGELICALISM

The heart of evangelicalism is the conviction that Christ reveals himself to his people through the Word. The greatest treasure I have received from the fathers and mothers of my evangelical heritage as they "brought me up" in the truths of the faith is a love for the Word of God. I remember Mike McClymond, a senior who had better things to do, dropping by my fraternity during exam week to make sure I was going to study Philippians with him during the next quarter. I remember Campus Crusade staff member Rich Blue teaching me how to use a commentary. I remember Sandi and I agreeing during our junior year in college to read the Bible every day the following year. I remember sitting in the chapel of John MacArthur's church with five hundred other pastors and watching in awe at how he handled the Word. I remember feelings of mystery and reverence the first time I read a verse out of my Greek New Testament. I remember the legendary reputation of Professor Fineberg who revered the Bible so much he would set no other book on top of it. I remember when venerable Dr. Christian, our history professor, shared with us the worst mistake he ever made: "Preaching when I wasn't prepared."

And I gave my life to passing this legacy on to the next generation.

JESUS SPEAKS

Talking, communicating, revealing, speaking, engaging, expressing, calling life into being—this is the essence of who Jesus is. Jesus said, "Man does not live on bread alone, but on every word that comes from the mouth of God."[1] We have those words recorded for us in Scripture. They bring us life, shared life in Christ. "My sheep listen to my voice," Jesus stated. "I know them, and they follow me."[2]

Words are the bridges over which two people journey into relationship. You are reading my words. My prayer is that by reading them you are sharing part of my heart—that we, as reader and writer, are forming a relationship.

Without words, relationships are nearly impossible. A friend of mine works with autistic children. They come to her in a wordless world, locked in a prison of silence, incapable of relating to anyone but themselves. Healing comes for these children, my friend tells me, when they learn to speak. Speech connects them with community. Healing occurs as they learn how to form and share their own words and hear words from others. Words rebuild the bridge blown apart by their disorder.

Imagine, for just a moment, any scene where two people are in relationship: a grandfather baiting his grandson's fish hook, two preschoolers building a fort in a sandbox, senior citizens happily chatting over dinner in their retirement center, young lovers holding one another beneath a mossy bridge, a college son calling home on Mother's Day. Words are the currency of each of these relationships.

Without words, relationships are nearly impossible.

Words are equally important in our relationship with Jesus Christ. Jesus is the Word. "His name," John tells us, "is the Word of God."[3] He is the expression of God's heart. He is the bridge over which we journey into relationship with God. He is the currency of our relationship with the Divine.

A DANCING FATHER

The Word is the Father's voice to his children.

My daughters love to hear my voice. They love to put their hands on my lips and feel the breath pass over their fingers when I say their name or sing a bedtime song or tell them how much I love them. When I misuse my father's voice and speak harshly to them, their faces twist with pain, and tears fill their eyes. A father's voice is a powerful shaping force in a young girl's life. "All I ever wanted to hear Daddy say," a female friend told me once in a moment of painful insight, "was that he loved me." Healing comes for a daughter of the King when she begins to hear her Father's voice speak to her in the Word. When his voice begins to speak into her life more powerfully than the other voices in her life, she begins to discover who she really is and to fall more deeply in love with the Father who delights in her.

Sandi and I once led a workshop on sacred dance for a number of women in our church. I had the women read Zephaniah 3:17 aloud:

He will take great delight in you,
He will quiet you with his love
He will rejoice over you with singing.

I shared with them that the Hebrew word for "rejoice" literally means "dance."

"Take a moment now and imagine the Father dancing over you," I said. The Father's voice of affirmation began to speak through his Word. He began to speak so intimately into the wounds of a number of the women that we had to delay the rest of the conference and pray for each other. Woman after woman shared that these were words they had always longed to hear from their fathers, but never had. The voice of the Father was healing them.

IRON JOHN

Sons, like daughters, also need to hear the Father's voice. Young men do not become mature men unless they do. One of the developmental tasks every boy faces is to be "called out" by his father's voice. He must leave the world of his mother and be accepted into the world of men. His earthly father—and then his heavenly Father—plays a key role in this transition.

Poet Robert Bly's book *Iron John* swept the country a few years back, helping ignite a national men's movement, including a lot of jokes about male bonding. Yet there was some truth to what he wrote. The book is based on the Grimm's fairy tale "Iron John" in which a hairy, wild man hides at the bottom of a forest lake and leaps out to seize men as they walk by. The Wild Man, who is named Iron John, is eventually captured by the king's men and forced to live in the center of the village in a cage. One day the king's son accidentally lets his golden ball role into the Wild Man's cage.

> The boy ran to the cage and said, "Give me my golden ball."
>
> "Not until you've opened the door for me," the man answered.
>
> The next day the boy returned and asked for his ball again. The Wild Man said, "If you open the door," but the boy would not. On the third day, while the King was out hunting, the boy came once again, and said, "Even if I wanted to, I couldn't open the lock because I don't have the key." The Wild Man said, "The key is under your mother's pillow; you can retrieve it."[4]

The boy steals the key from under his mother's pillow and lives with the Wild Man in the forest until he grows up. The boy, now a man, eventually rescues a nearby kingdom and marries the king's daughter. He has become a man.

This story, according to Bly, describes the journey every boy must take into the world of men. The Wild Man represents the voice of the Father, the True Masculine, who calls the boy away from his mother and into the world of men. The boy in the fairy tale "steals the key from his mother's pillow" and walks with Iron John into the world of men. He is now able to conquer kingdoms and bond appropriately with a woman in marriage.

Bly's vision of manhood and the process boys must take to become men resonates with most men I know. We enter the world looking for the voice that will call us into the world of men. We look to our fathers for this affirmation; but even in this, we look beyond them to a deeper voice, the voice of the heavenly Father.

Jesus, at the moment he began his public ministry, heard the Father's voice. "This is my Son, whom I love," the voice said. "With him I am well pleased."[5] This is the voice every boy and girl longs to hear.

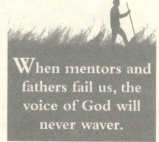

What are we looking for the voice to say? Words of affirmation. Words of guidance. Words of hope. We can hear these words from our fathers and from mentors— and this is a good thing. But nothing can substitute for hearing the voice of God thunder from the Word: "This is my beloved son. This is my beloved daughter. With them I am well pleased." And when mentors and fathers fail us, the voice of God will never waver.

When mentors and fathers fail us, the voice of God will never waver.

The cry of the prophets to ancient Israel was, "Come here and listen to the words of the LORD your God."[6] How do we hear the word of the Lord in Scripture?

JESUS REVEALED THROUGH SCRIPTURE

When we open our Bibles, we are not merely reading a great book. We must prepare to encounter the living Christ. Scripture reveals the person of Jesus Christ. Shortly after his resurrection, Jesus joined two of his discouraged disciples on the Emmaus Road and taught them from Scripture. "And beginning with Moses and all the Prophets, he explained to them what was said in all the Scriptures *concerning himself.*" Scripture reveals Jesus. The church father Origen said that in the incarnation, the Son of God became a man; in Scripture, he became a book. Origen may have gone a bit too far with his illustration, but his point is absolutely correct— Scripture is much more than a mere book. The words of Scripture express the living Christ.

Martin Luther agrees with Origin when he writes, "Holy Scripture is the garment which our Lord Jesus Christ has put on and in which he lets himself be found."

We must expect a fresh, dynamic word from Jesus. We must pray for a revelation from Christ that explodes into our worlds and jars us wide awake.

THE MIRACLE OF PREACHING

We encounter this living word when the Word is preached. Shortly after my conversion I began to attend a church pastored by Jim Custer, a gifted expositor. I had never heard anyone open the Word like Pastor Jim. Sometimes, even as a fifteen-year-old, I would sit through the service twice just to hear the sermon again. The words on the page began to dance when Pastor Jim preached. More than once I was certain he had called my mother and found out what I had struggled with that week, since his sermons always hit a personal chord. I would walk home from church in reverent silence. Jesus had spoken. And I had heard his voice. This is the miracle of preaching.

I preached my senior sermon in seminary on 1 Timothy 4:6: "If you point these things [sound doctrine] out to the brothers, you will be a good minister of Christ Jesus, brought up in the truths of the faith and of the good teaching that you have followed." God's presence was uniquely present in our seminary chapel that day, and I experienced for the first time what the Puritans called "unction" in preaching: a unique awareness of God's presence and power in the preaching of the Word.

Ever since my first experience, I enjoy nothing more than preaching the Word of God. Somehow, God speaks—actually *speaks*—to thousands of people each Sunday through me as I preach the Word of God. I made a vow in seminary never to stand in the pulpit unless I was sure I had heard a fresh word from the Lord. It has cost me a lot to keep this vow, and many Saturday nights have found me desperately pacing the worship center asking God to breathe life into the dead words of my sermon manuscript. I am sure I have had my share of off Sundays, yet I am continually amazed, week in and week out, at the power of the preached Word of God. The preached Word heals, saves, convicts, comforts, and guides. God's story faithfully preached begins to shape our own stories. The preached Word becomes the voice of the Father, calling us into the full men and women he wants us to become.

READING THE VOICE OF GOD

Good relationships require conversation, and conversation requires listening to another person's words. The way we begin conversation with God is by reading his words. When we pick up Scripture we are beginning a dialogue with God. The conversational nature of Scripture reading is important to keep in mind because our tendency is to approach the Bible looking for facts instead of a relationship. We are trained to read literature "critically," to sit objectively outside of the text and study it until we have mastered its material. The point of reading the Bible, however, is to be mastered by the One who is the Word.

When we pick up Scripture we are beginning a dialogue with God.

The Holy Spirit inspired the authors of Scripture when they wrote the books of the Bible. Today, we need to invite the Spirit to breathe on Scripture in a fresh way so they come alive to *us*. A good prayer for the illumination of the Spirit is found in Ephesians 1:17: "I keep asking that the God of our Lord Jesus Christ, the glorious Father, may give you the Spirit of wisdom and revelation, so that you may know him better." You may want to pray Paul's prayer for yourself as you begin.

Now that you are ready to read, how much do you read? One Christian leader I know spent his vacation reading through the book of Acts once each day. Reading through the Bible in a year or taking a course in Old Testament survey has many benefits. For example, we are exposed to the great themes of Scripture; we become more familiar with the biblical worldview; and we gain a fuller appreciation of God's amazing faithfulness throughout history.

Listening-reading, however, has a different goal. We approach the text seeking to come away with the Word of the Lord for our day. Rather than reading an entire chapter of the Bible, select a paragraph, or even a sentence. Read it slowly, over and over again. Ask the Lord to highlight the word he has for you today. In my mind, I imagine my passage on a computer screen. I ask the Lord to boldface the verses that he wants me to focus on during the day. You may find that the Lord has you stay in the same passage for a number of days. Dietrich Bonhoeffer urged his disciples to spend a whole week on just one verse.

Again, read slowly. One master of the spiritual life cautions against the danger of reading too fast: "If you read quickly, it will benefit you little. You will be like a bee that merely skims the surface of the flower. Instead . . . you must become as the bee who penetrates into the depths of the flower. You must plunge within to remove its deepest nectar."[8]

It is very possible, though, to know the Bible cover to cover without ever encountering the living Word. Pastors know all too well that we can master what the Bible teaches without being mastered by the Teacher. One afternoon in seminary I walked out of Greek class and saw a large crowd of students gathered around an old, white van. My seminary was not prone toward student gatherings, so I walked over to take a look. The van was full of books, which a disheveled-looking man was stacking on tables on the campus sidewalk. Word had spread that he had books for sale, and that he was letting them go cheap. Like most seminarians, I was attracted to cheap books like moths are to light, so I lingered in the back of the crowd, eyeing a massive set of *Kittel's Theological Dictionary* and wondering what the van driver would let it go for.

"Anybody know why this guy is selling books so cheap? Where did he get them, anyway?" I asked a classmate.

"Some pastor up in the valley," he replied. "He lost his faith and doesn't want anything to do with the ministry anymore."

I passed up the good deal on Kittel.

Studying the Bible and encountering the living Christ are not necessarily the same thing—as that pastor tragically found out. We can be in Scripture and not know Christ.

REFLECTING ON SCRIPTURE

Reflection takes the word you have read and downloads it into your heart. Reflecting on a passage turns reading into listening. Reflection is another word for the biblical term "meditation." Meditation is mentioned more than fifty times in the Bible. Isaac heads out to a field to meditate.[9] David speaks of meditation when he writes, "On my bed I remember you; I think of you through the watches of the night."[10] Mary meditated when she "pondered . . . in her heart" the word from the Lord about her child.[11] Reflection turns principles into personal words for our lives from the Lord.

One afternoon while traveling in another city I stopped by an art store to browse. One particular painting caught my eye. The painting was a winter landscape set in the west. Muscular brown horses peered out from behind birch trees clustered tightly together in a snow-covered wood. Yet there was more to the painting than what I was seeing—it had a scent of mystery about it. The store clerk eventually came by and asked me what I saw.

> Reflection turns principles into personal words for our lives from the Lord.

"It's a painting of horses among birch trees in the woods," I said.

"Look again," she told me.

I did, and still saw nothing.

"Don't you see the Indians?" she asked.

Suddenly, my eyes were opened and I could see a dozen Indians hiding behind the trees. It took the help of the clerk to make me aware of the reality hidden in the painting. Listening-reading is like that. We need the help of the Holy Spirit to open our eyes to what God wants us to see in the passage.

One definition of the Hebrew word for meditation is "chewing the cud." Reflection is simply chewing over and over a biblical word, phrase, or sentence until its meaning has seeped into the spiritual digestive system.

"Any serious reading of the Bible means personal involvement with it, not simply agreement with abstract propositions," writes Thomas Merton.[12] This is an important step in hearing the voice of the Lord in Scripture. We must intentionally press beyond facts and allow the Word to intersect with our experience. This is why many find journaling a helpful way to begin the reflective process. By sharing our feelings and concerns with the Lord in writing, we prepare the soil of our hearts for the seed of the living Word.

RESPONDING TO WHAT WE HEAR

Building a relationship when all of the words flow one way is difficult. Dialogue involves communication from both parties: words, and a response to words. Have you ever known someone who talks too much without giving you a chance to respond? Or, have you ever shared a thought you felt was either revealing or profound, only to have the person listening just stare at you? It is unnerving. Good conversationalists know how to "complete the loop" when words are spoken.

In a similar way, we need to "complete the loop" when God has spoken to us through his Word. The Word of God always demands a response. When God talks, talk back. A comforting word draws forth a response of thanksgiving. A convicting word moves us to repentance. A word about the beauty of Christ leads us to praise. A word of what might be moves us to cry out over what really is.

HEARING THE MESSAGE

A month after our Solemn Assembly, the guys in my men's accountability group took our annual fishing trip. This year Randi, the true sports fisherman of the group, decided we needed to head for the Outer Banks of South Carolina and fish for bluefin tuna off Cape Hatteras.

The timing could not have been better. The church was beginning to heal from the surgery we experienced during the Solemn Assembly— but the process was slow. I was leading a restructuring process and hitting walls at every turn. We were having a hard time moving again. I was stumped—and ready to get away.

The first day on the Outer Banks we decided to lay low and not fish. It was a sunny, brisk November day, the kind summer vacationers rarely have the pleasure of experiencing. After breakfast I found a deserted spot on the beach and began to write in my journal, sharing with the Lord my confusion and frustration. My reading plan had me in 2 Samuel 6, where a poor fellow named Uzzah is struck dead because he tried to steady the ark. *Great,* I thought. *This devotion is really going to warm my heart.*

Then I began to hear the voice of Jesus speak through his Word. Flipping back and forth, studying what the Bible had to say about the ark and how it should be handled, I was reminded that only Levites were allowed to handle the ark. God had promised severe punishments for anyone touching the ark who was not a member of Levi's tribe, no matter what their intentions might have been.

Uzzah was not a Levite. He was a good guy doing a job God had not called him to do. And he died doing it.

I set my Bible by my chair, took another sip of coffee, and stared past the Cape Hatteras lighthouse as a soft breeze turned the pages of my journal. Jesus was speaking: "When you put the right guy in the wrong place, you kill him."

That word guided me through an entire year of a challenging organizational change. I remembered that word as I sat at my computer and wrote the elders my letter. I remembered that word when we struggled to find the right place for the right guy. I remembered that word when the pressures of the moment nearly forced us to put the right person in the wrong place.

Even now, as I let my mind drift back to that sun-swept hour near the Cape Hatteras lighthouse, my heart is warmed. Jesus cared for me. Jesus spoke into my world. And I heard.

HAVE I HEARD YOU?

"Have I heard you?" I asked Sandi one night at the end of a long conversation. "Yes," she smiled. "I really think you have." And we hugged.

When we hear our lover's heart, intimacy is the result.

FIVE

PROPHETIC WHISPERS

Vision is conceived when we are intimate with Jesus. He impregnates with the seed of his vision, which we carry and then give birth to. A major reason why I am writing this book is because too few of God's people have discovered his vision for their lives. We do not understand that just as a husband and wife cannot conceive a child without becoming intimate, we cannot birth God's vision in our hearts if we are not intimate with him.

Once a vision is conceived, though, it must be nourished and encouraged or it will die. The seed that implants God's vision in the womb of our inner world is the Word of God. When God's story intersects with our story, vision is born. This is one way in which every human being is the bride while the Son is the Bridegroom. He is always the one who penetrates us with the seed of his Word and impregnates us with his vision. We are the receivers of the vision, the carriers of it.

Vision born, however, is not vision fulfilled.

FADING VISIONS

Tina, a young mother of three, clings to a vision of what her family can become. Her husband does not share the vision. Bit by bit, year by year, Tina's vision slowly fades: the days are too long; the thank-yous are too few.

Brian, a junior in college, felt his heart shatter for the people of Vietnam one Sunday in church. He stands when the pastor asks if anyone senses a call to serve overseas. Yet Brian is deeply in debt. He begins working to pay off his loans, but finds his meager salary is barely enough to pay his bills. Then, Brian marries. He has children. He buys a home. His salary increases but so do his responsibilities. Brian's twenties slip into his thirties, and his vision for the Vietnamese slowly slips away. Brian feels a part of him die every time he thinks about the calling he has not fulfilled.

Tom has not heard from his eldest daughter Cindy in four years. Cindy has been a tremendous disappointment to him. She began hanging around with the wrong crowd in high school, got pregnant in college, dropped out, and now lives with her toddler and two other single moms in a doublewide trailer somewhere in New Mexico. Tom is haunted by their last conversation.

"You've never accepted me," Cindy shouted, throwing clothes into a suitcase. "Nothing I ever did was good enough." He has not seen or heard from her since. A year ago God began to speak to Tom about reconciling with Cindy. For six months every time Tom opened the Bible, heard a sermon, or went to a Bible study he heard the same message: call your daughter and tell her you love her. Yet Tom has not called. The vision for reconciliation has not yet conquered the pain and rejection Tom feels in his own heart. The brokenness Tom felt a year ago is slowly turning into numbness. He is allowing God's vision to fade away. And he knows it.

Tina, Brian, and Tom are watching their visions slowly die. Vision born is not vision fulfilled.

Re-visioning in Ephesus

Timothy, the young church planter we get to know in Paul's letters to him, was losing his vision. Ephesus was a difficult mission field, ripe with occult activity, and Timothy was applying for a transfer.

Paul wrote his young protégé to rekindle his dying vision. And he asked Timothy to remember the prophecies spoken over him at his commissioning. "Timothy, my son," Paul pleads. "I give you this instruction in keeping with the prophecies once made about you, so that by following them you may fight the good fight."[1]

Prophecy stirs the waning flames of our vision and encourages us to fight the good fight. "Everyone who prophecies speaks to men for their strengthening, encouragement, and comfort,"[2] Paul reminds us.

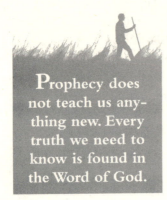

Prophecy does not teach us anything new. Every truth we need to know is found in the Word of God.

Prophecy does not teach us anything new. Every truth we need to know is found in the Word of God. Prophetic words remind us of what the voice has already said, and encourage us to obey. Prophecy reminds us of our calling—our destiny— and plugs the holes where our vision is leaking. Prophecy teaches us to see not what is, but what could be. Prophecy takes our eyes off our present reality and paints a picture of God's intended future reality.

ENCOURAGEMENT FROM AN UNLIKELY PLACE

I have a vision. You have bumped into part of it in this book. I believe that we are at one of the most critical points in the history of Western civilization as the modern age gives way to the postmodern age. This is a time of terror. It is also a time of great opportunity for the Gospel. Postmodern people are ravenously hungry for God. They are seeking a God they can both know intellectually and experience intimately. I am convinced that God is bringing together the two rivers of Word and power spirituality to birth one united church throbbing with spiritual power and saturated with God's eternal truth. My first book, *The Word and Power Church,* shares this vision in detail. I would like to share with you the vision I wrote about in *The Word and Power Church.*

> Think of the charismatic and evangelical traditions as two mighty spiritual rivers flowing through our century. Today the two rivers are merging into one mighty flood of spiritual power. God is blending the strengths of both the evangelical and charismatic traditions together in churches across America. I call these *word and power churches.* . . .
>
> These are not days to be complacent. Our nation is at a critical juncture and is poised to reject the Christian faith forever. Dare we go about business as usual? Dare we ignore what Christians have to offer one another? Could it be that God raised up both evangelical and charismatic traditions in our time because a

healthy, vibrant church needs what we both have learned about spiritual life and ministry? Could it be that God has raised up both evangelical and charismatic traditions because he knew that the post-Christian mission field we are called to conquer craves a God of Truth and Power?[3]

This is my vision. More than once, the vision has nearly died. Not everyone agrees with me when I say that I believe both charismatic and evangelical spirituality are equally true. Pursuing this vision has cost me friendships and reputation. Birthing this vision in our church was not easy, and we did not always lead into the vision well. It will not be easy taking this vision to the nations. But I have heard the voice. And I cannot go back.

I have encountered the tender, nurturing side of my heavenly Father through his prophetic gift. Like young Timothy, I often remember the prophetic words spoken over me when the winds of discouragement threaten to snuff out the flames of my vision.

My vision for unity among these "two tribes" was refined during my graduate work and became the subject for my doctoral dissertation. Part of my dissertation work included a two-week period of research at a Pentecostal college. I felt it was necessary to read about Pentecostalism from its own point of view to fully appreciate the movement. I also attended Pentecostal worship services and interviewed students, pastors, and professors. One professor had a reputation as a prophet, and nearly everyone I spoke with encouraged me to meet with him. He had a Ph.D. in Old Testament from Vanderbilt and a good reputation as a scholar. When I entered his office, he was working on a translation of the book of Job. My categories were blurring—somehow I could not put together a Vanderbilt Ph.D. with the title "prophet." In those days, I realize now, I was still living under the prejudice that experiential believers could not be thinking believers. We spoke at length about his tradition, how he fled from it and then returned. Then, at the end of our hour together, I asked him if he had a prophetic word for me. He thought for a moment, and then nodded.

"Bridge builder," he said. "You will be a bridge builder between the evangelical and Pentecostal worlds."

Like young Timothy, I have thought of that word often, especially when my vision fades or circumstances rise up against its fulfillment.

What Is Prophecy?

What is prophecy? The gift of prophecy is a spontaneous, divinely given insight into a person, event, or situation. We see the gift in action in Paul's letter to the Corinthians:

> If an unbeliever or someone who does not understand comes in while everybody is prophesying, he will be convinced by all that he is a sinner and will be judged by all, and the secrets of his heart will be laid bare. So he will fall down and worship God, exclaiming, "God is really among you!"[4]

When the prophetic word is shared, it ministers to the person and causes those present to praise God. The Greek word for "laid bare" means "to reveal."[5] Prophecy is supernatural revelation. We receive from the Holy Spirit information we would have no natural way of knowing. The supernatural nature of this communication leaves everyone involved sensing that "God is among us." The people receiving the prophetic word are drawn closer to God, even to the point of falling down and worshiping. Why? Because the God of the heavens just broke into their world and spoke personally to them.

Facing Fears

Like many evangelicals, I was suspicious at first of the possibility of God speaking personally to me. It seemed dangerous. Isn't it possible that I might misunderstand Jesus? Gradually, I have realized that these same fears apply to any relationship. Sandi and I often miss one another when we communicate, though less now than in the early days of our marriage. Sandi and I could choose to communicate only by writing. That way, we would have a written record of everything we said. There would be less chance of misunderstanding each other. We would also kill our marriage, especially if we only wrote one extensive letter to one another at the beginning and then just referred back to it when we had any questions! A healthy marriage needs written communication, but it also needs spontaneous, intimate, daily interaction. The same is true with our relationship with Christ.

Every kingdom is built on both forms of communication. Kingdoms have objective revelation: revered written words explaining the vision for the kingdom and the rules of the kingdom. These written words also warn of the dangers of violating the laws of the kingdom and touch upon the rewards for keeping those laws. Knowing this objective revelation is crucial for good citizenship in the kingdom.

Kingdoms also have subjective revelation in which the king communicates personally to his subjects on contemporary matters that the constitution did not and could not cover.

The same is true within the kingdom of God. Scripture describes the vision and laws of the kingdom. The King, however, is still actively reigning over his kingdom and regularly speaks to his subjects to help them apply kingdom laws in their daily lives.

It seems only reasonable to believe that our King, Jesus Christ, did not finish speaking when the Bible was finished being written. "We think a silent God suddenly began to speak in a book and when the book was finished lapsed into silence again forever," wrote A. W. Tozer. "With notions like that in our heads how can we believe?"[6]

THE PROPHETIC PROMISE

Jesus anticipates this rich, interpersonal, communicative friendship with his followers at the Last Supper. He is very careful to state three different times that his followers can and must expect an ongoing dialogue with him after the resurrection.

"But when he, the Spirit of truth, comes, he will guide you into all truth. He will not speak on his own; he will speak only what he hears. . . . The Spirit will take from what is mine and make it known to you."[7]

Charismatic spirituality reminds us that one way the Spirit breathes the words of Christ to us today is through the prophetic. Jesus is our Good Shepherd. He knows when our vision is dying. He knows when we need a prophetic word.

THE VISION WILL NOT DIE

When our church went through its year of pain I feared that the vision we had worked so hard to build might relapse into sickness because of our own sins and mistakes. How could this be? God had brought us so far. How could I write and speak about unity and renewal when our own church was in relational turmoil? God used the prophetic to keep the vision burning.

I shared with you in chapter 2 that the "final blow" to the tenuous health I clung to was my friend's painful but truthful letter. It takes me a while to work through criticism and really hear what God is saying through it. I know now that God was working through the letter to apply the principle I learned at Cape Hatteras—good guys in the wrong places get themselves killed. It was time for this Uzzah to change roles. Today, my new role is much better suited to my gifts and allows me to further the vision with much greater freedom. But I did not see that then. Instead, I thought my vision had received another deadly blow.

A few days after receiving the letter, I spoke at a retreat center in the mountains outside Knoxville. After the message, everyone except one couple quickly disappeared. I sensed that the Father was working in the couple, and the three of us began to talk.[8] The Father *was* working, and we simply joined him in prayer as the Holy Spirit revealed some lies in the wife's heart that had crippled her spiritually for many years. We prayed for emotional and spiritual healing, and the Spirit gently ministered to her.

It was about midnight, but we were not through yet. One of the lies that this woman had come to believe had to do with hearing God speak. She had concluded that she was not godly enough or mature enough to hear his voice even though earlier in her Christian life she had learned to hear God's voice quite clearly. We addressed this deception in prayer and asked the Spirit to awaken a dormant prophetic gift in her life. She began to quietly prophesy—to share what God was spontaneously putting on her mind.

"I'm not sure what this means," she said. "But this is what I am hearing. . . . The vision will not die, Doug. I think God wants to encourage you and let you know the vision will not die."

"You don't know what you just did for me, my friend," I said, hugging them both. She had no idea what I had dealt with that week. Jesus, out of his compassionate, tender heart, had given her a personal word just for me. I felt overtaken by his shepherd's heart for me—he had arranged all of this, just because he knew I needed encouragement.

"You're kidding," she said, wiping away tears. "I can't believe God would use me that way." I was not the only one touched by the power of the prophetic that night. She too was touched that God would use her to bring a word that spoke into the mystery of a brother's heart.

THE CHURCH AS A PROPHETIC COMMUNITY

The prophets of old yearned for the day when everyone would be able to walk as intimately with God as they did. Moses once cried out, "I wish that all the LORD's people were prophets and that the LORD would put his Spirit on them!"[9] They peered into the future and saw a day when the Spirit would birth a prophetic community, marked by the universal ability to hear God's voice in dreams, visions, and prophetic words. God predicted this new, Spirit-drenched, prophetic community through the prophet Joel:

> "I will pour out my Spirit on all people.
> Your sons and daughters will prophesy,
> > your old men will dream dreams,
> > your young men will see visions.
> Even on my servants, both men and women,
> > I will pour out my Spirit in those days."[10]

I had read that verse hundreds of times and had never before seen the significance of the prophetic within it. The lights began to go on when I read Mike Bickle's book *Growing in the Prophetic*.[11] He helped me see that we are a prophetic people, even as we are a people of the Word. "In the church at Antioch there were prophets and teachers,"[12] Luke records. These believers were hearing the voice of Jesus, through teachers of the Word and through the prophetic ministry.

Presently our city is enjoying the fruits of a growing pastors' prayer movement. We meet regularly for prayer in small groups all across the city and then gather once a year for a four-day Prayer Summit. I have learned a great deal from these pastors. My charismatic pastor-friends have taught me a lot about the prophetic ministry. I have prayed with them enough to know that the prophetic comes alongside the Word and does not replace it. My fears about the abuse of this gift have greatly subsided as I have walked with these men.

GO AND LOOK

Some prophetic words clarify vision. Some prophetic words give guidance. One evening as the elders were praying before we started working through a long agenda, a silence fell—and no one rushed to fill it. We sensed that God wanted to speak. After a long pause, one of the elders said, "I can't get Kosovo off my mind." The war in Kosovo was at its height. "I think I'm hearing the Lord say, 'Go and look.'" God touched our heart for the refugees from Kosovo—a group of Albanian Muslims with almost no gospel witness. What happened next had never happened in any of our elder prayer meetings. Within moments, some elders were lying on the floor, some crying, others standing next to a world map to lay hands on Yugoslavia to intercede with great passion. None of this, of course, was on the agenda and we had not discussed ministering in Kosovo prior to this evening. When the evening had finished, God had birthed a vision in our heart for reaching the Kosovars. As I write, a ministry team from our church is in Albania, exploring ways to make contact with the tiny remnant of believers in Kosovo. The evening reminded us of a similar elders meeting in the Antioch church when "the Holy Spirit said, 'Set apart for me Barnabas and Saul for the work to which I have called them.'"[13]

INTIMACY IN ACTS

I cannot help but believe that the believers in the book of Acts felt very intimate with the risen Lord Jesus. He had spoken when he was on earth and he continued to speak through the prophetic and through the Word. The book of Acts records the fulfillment of Christ's promise to continue speaking to his Church: The Spirit tells Philip to minister to the Ethiopian eunuch.[14] Jesus appears to Paul in a vision and begins his conversion process.[15] Ananias has a vision preparing him to greet the newly converted Paul.[16] Peter falls into a trance while praying and sees a vision that reveals to him that all foods are clean.[17] Agabus accurately prophesies a famine.[18] The Holy Spirit speaks to the church at Antioch, telling them to send out Barnabas and Paul (Saul).[19] The Holy Spirit keeps Paul from preaching in Asia.[20] During the night, Paul has a vision of a man from Macedonia pleading for help; Paul's missionary team immediately responds.[21] Paul experiences another night vision in which the Lord tells him he will be protected from harm and that many people are prepared for the Gospel in Corinth.[22] The Ephesian believers speak in tongues and prophesy when Paul lays hands on them.[23] Paul is compelled by the Spirit to go to Jerusalem; the Spirit warns him that prison and hardships face him.[24] Luke notes that Philip the evangelist has four unmarried daughters who prophesied.[25] The prophet Agabus prophesies that the Jews will turn Paul over to the Gentiles.[26] The Lord appears to Paul while he is held prisoner in Jerusalem to encourage him that his ministry is not finished yet.[27]

We cannot conclude that the early church experienced a continuous stream of supernatural revelations. These examples are taken from a generation of ministry of the leading figures of the post-resurrection church. Certainly there were "dark nights of the soul" when God did not speak. Certainly some believers and some churches experienced more supernatural communication than others. Yet even allowing for these qualifications, Luke's agenda is hard to miss: Jesus still speaks to his church. Luke begins the book of Acts remarking that in his first book, the gospel of Luke, he wrote about "all that Jesus *began* to do and teach."[28] The book of Acts, then, records what Jesus *continues* to do and teach, through his Spirit.

The church in Acts had a keen sense of the personal presence of their Lord. "Everyone," Luke observes, "was filled with awe."[29] Much of this awe, no doubt, came from the powerful, anointed preaching of the Word. Yet the almost eerie sense of God's immediacy can also be attributed to the frequent occurrence of supernatural revelation—pinpoint accurate, personal communication from a living, reigning Christ who is very much still in charge of his church.

PRAYING AND THE PROPHETIC

I feel very close to God when he speaks into my life prophetically. How can it be that the Creator of the universe has enough time to care about what I am thinking and feeling and struggling with? God's wounded children often feel embraced by him when those who pray for them speak prophetic words into the sore spots of their hearts.

I was recently praying for a friend who has been experiencing heart problems. I was praying general prayers for his health and spiritual well-being when God seemed to break into my prayers to add a thought of his own.

"It's his weight," I sensed God say.

I was reluctant to talk to my friend about such a sensitive matter and wanted to make sure I had truly heard from the Lord, so I held onto the word for several days. Finally, I called him.

"I've been praying about your heart," I told him.

"And. . ." he said tentatively.

"This is a little personal. But I think the Lord may be saying that your heart problem has something to do with you being just a bit heavy."

> How can it be that the Creator of the universe has enough time to care about what I am thinking and feeling and struggling with?

There was a long pause. I wondered if I had gone too far. "Astounding," he said. "You are the third person who has told me that in two days. One guy came over to my house this afternoon just to share the same word with me. I guess God's trying to say something, don't you think?"

A week later, I checked in. "I feel so loved by God through all this," he shared with me after discussing his new diet and exercise plans. "I feel really shepherded—God loves me enough to send you guys to bring a word like that. Wow!"

Leanne was praying for her friend Donna when she heard the phrase "glaring eyes." Pausing, she looked at Donna and asked, "Does the phrase 'glaring eyes' mean anything to you?" They continued to pray. Donna realized that the key men in her life all looked at her through glaring eyes. She realized that she had assumed her heavenly father also looked at her through the same glaring eyes. This insight, combined with Leanne's gentle prayer and tender friendship, opened significant doors of healing in Donna's life. Donna's experience of the prophetic helped tear down her image of God as a Father with "glaring eyes."

Protecting Yourself from Prophetic Abuse

Not every prophetic word brings healing and warm feelings of intimacy with Christ. The prophetic gift, like every gift, can be abused. For many of us, walking in the prophetic is a relatively new discipline. Inevitably, we make mistakes and hurt one another. The natural tendency is to respond by choosing to never have anything to do with the prophetic again. Yet the Bible clearly forbids this response. "Do not treat prophecies with contempt," Paul flatly stated.[30]

We can protect ourselves from prophetic abuse by asking four questions when someone shares a word with us.

Is the content of the word biblical? "True prophecy gladly submits to the final authority of Scripture," explains George Mallone, "for it is not a new revelation of truth for the church but a harmonic expression of that truth."[31]

Is the word consistent with the spirit of Jesus? According to Revelation, "The testimony of Jesus is the spirit of prophecy."[32] A true prophetic word will sound like a word that Jesus might say.

Is the person speaking walking with God? Scripture is often more concerned with the character of the prophet than the words of the prophet. Jesus explicitly warns us of false prophets, urging us to discern their true nature by testing the fruit of their character.[33] This is why it is never a good idea to receive anonymous prophecy.

Is the word given in love? "If I have the gift of prophecy . . . but have not love," Paul writes, "I am nothing."[34]

The best safeguard, of course, from prophetic pain is a loving relationship. All spiritual gifts are practiced better in community. The gift of prophecy is no exception. If you really desire to grow in this gift and learn to hear God's voice speak to you this way, why not spend some time studying this gift with your small group? Then, as you begin to practice this gift, give feedback to one another about where you are. Give one another the freedom to fail, and hold one another accountable to keep Scripture as your ongoing, basic spiritual meal.

Whispers in the Night

Dreams are another way God speaks prophetically into our lives. "No communication," writes Ken Gire, "is as intimate, I think, as a dream whispered to our soul in the middle of the night."[35] The psalmist knew the night whispers of his Shepherd. "Even at night," he writes, "my heart instructs me."[36]

This past year I became ill with a lingering sickness that refused to be diagnosed or cured. It lasted one month, then two. Medicine did not touch it, and I began to wonder if something more serious was wrong.

All spiritual gifts are practiced better in community. The gift of prophecy is no exception.

One evening my elders prayed for healing for me. The next day, one of them called me and said that after praying for me he had gone to bed and God had given him a dream about me. Three different men appeared in the dream. Somehow, he had the sense that my sickness was linked to my relationship with them. He then shared the names of the three men. I winced. God had been putting these three men on my heart for some time, urging me to check in with them and make sure our relationship was in good shape. I am embarrassed to admit that I had been putting these appointments off. I met with the three men over the next ten days. The day after I met with the third man, my sickness disappeared.

God used a dream to bring about both relational and physical healing in my life. But more than that, his gracious intervention in my life in answer to my brother's prayer reminded me how much he cares for me.

SIX

PRAYER AND
BEING FATHERED

Sandi and I often plan our holiday trips so that we spend some time driving through the night. We find a restaurant that has a deal on kids' meals, fill up their little tummies, and then hit the road. By Atlanta, they are normally out cold.

We pour a cup of coffee, turn on a favorite CD, and settle in for a long talk. Often we have not connected in a while and have much to share. Sandi normally begins by sharing with me the cares of the week. Then, as the miles and moments roll by, she gives me the gift of her heart. Her words descend the staircase of intimacy, and we reach places of communion that are all too rare in our busy life.

Inevitably, I long to share my heart with her, too. Sometimes we interact point-by-point, weaving the threads of our stories into one. On other nights, she talks until she is through, and then I talk until I am through. Good conversations are like that. They evoke a response.

Watch people who love each other have a conversation. Their words create a dance of voice—their sentences weaving, bowing, stepping in and out, carefully avoiding stepping on the other. Watch the subtle interplay of initiative and response: laughter evokes laughter; tears bring forth tears.

Bad relationships, on the other hand, are relationships where conversation does not reciprocate. Certain images immediately come to mind: a mother reading a magazine while her daughter talks about her day. A marine drill sergeant screaming at a tight-lipped recruit. The exasperated words of a wife who has nearly given up communicating with a husband forever lost in his own distant world—"You're not listening to me!"

Healthy relationships enjoy dialogue between the partners. Both listen. And both speak. The same is true in our relationship with Jesus. Our conversational relationship with him begins, to be sure, with learning to listen to his voice. But it does not end there. The next task is learning how to speak in such a way that he hears us. The process of sharing our hearts with God is simply called prayer.

Evangelicals and charismatics have much to teach us about a vital prayer life. Evangelicals have given the church a heritage of rich preaching, writing, and practice in the life of prayer. Charismatics, equally committed to prayer, also have much to say to us about praying in a personal prayer language. All agree that prayer is essentially relationship. "Prayer," writes George Buttrick, "is friendship with God."[1]

A TARNISHED IMAGE

Susan Howatch's novel *Glittering Images* chronicles the spiritual meltdown and recovery of a thirty-seven-year-old Anglican priest named Charles Ashworth. Dr. Ashworth, a Cambridge theologian and promising protégé of the Archbishop of Canterbury, has many hidden skeletons in his closet that fall out about halfway through the book. When his carefully polished Glittering Image becomes tarnished, Ashworth experiences a spiritual and emotional breakdown and is sent to an Anglican monastery to recover. The broken cleric is given a mysterious monk named Father Darrow as his spiritual director who begins to peel back the layers of Ashworth's Glittering Image, exposing the bent longings of his heart.

God speaks to me through novels—and he spoke to me through this one. I have not fallen into all of the same sins Charles Ashworth has, but I have spent a lifetime polishing a Glittering Image and experienced its collapse. I read the book shortly after our Solemn Assembly when I experienced my own meltdown. Ashworth's healing became intertwined with my own healing, and some parts of his therapeutic dialogue with Darrow are now underlined in blue ink and permanently marked by a dog-eared page and a business card.

Ashworth discovered that much of what drove him into ministry was a desire to please father figures.

> "Charles, would I be reading too much into your remarks if I deduced that liking and approval are very important to you?"
>
> That was an easy question to answer. "Well, of course they are important!" I exclaimed. "Aren't they important to everyone? Isn't that what life's all about? Success is people liking and approving of you. Failure is being rejected. Everyone knows that."
>
> ". . .let's talk about all these father-figures you have accumulated over the years. . . . How would you yourself describe all these benign older men in your life?"
>
> . . . Regarding him with suspicion, I said austerely: "I hardly collect fathers for pleasure."[2]

"Benign older men" have a place, even a critical place, in our lives. Yet they cannot take the place of the Father God. One of the most significant tasks of our spiritual development is learning how to be fathered by God.

BEING FATHERED

Being fathered is the heart of prayer. "This, then, is how you should pray," Jesus taught his followers. "Our Father. . ."[3] When the disciples did not quite understand, Jesus used another father illustration:

> **One of the most significant tasks of our spiritual development is learning how to be fathered by God.**

> Which of you fathers, if your son asks for a fish, will give him a snake instead? Or if he asks for an egg, will give him a scorpion? If you then, though you are evil, know how to give good gifts to your children, how much more will your Father in heaven give the Holy Spirit to those who ask him!"[4]

Prayer is conversation between a child and a father.

I pastor a church teeming with fatherless young men and young women. The casualties of growing up fatherless are real and mounting. Yet there is hope. We can teach them to pray—because in prayer, the fatherless find a Father.

Evangelical spirituality is a spirituality of prayer. My shelves are filled with dozens of books by evangelical authors on prayer. Each of them points us to a Father who invites us to talk with him.

PRAYER AS PARTNERSHIP

Why does the Father want to hear what we have to say? Why, irony of ironies, does he humble himself to partner with us in saving the world? The answer is in one word: intimacy. He wants to know us and desires for us to know him. The Father invites us to *ask* him to bring about his kingdom on earth, as it is in the Father's kingdom. "Life is war," writes John Piper. "Prayer is primarily a wartime walkie-talkie for the mission of the church as it advances against the powers of darkness and unbelief."[5]

This wartime prayer partnership forges the deepest bond between us and our heavenly Father. Together we share in the rise and fall of the kingdom of God. Listen to the men who fought with Patton or MacArthur in World War II. Together they prevailed. They formed a bond with their commanding general as they partnered with him in making war. Prayer is a similar partnership. Prayer is "talking with God about what we are doing together."[6]

Every Thursday I fast and pray in a cabin overlooking the Tennessee River. I end the day walking in the woods and praying through the different battlefronts our church is facing. I have taken walks like these every Thursday now for seven years. It is on these quiet walks that my Father and I wage war. "Ask me to do through you what I want to do," the Father says—and I ask. I ask for the things that are on my heart. I ask about my children and I ask about my wife. I ask about my staff and I ask about my neighbors. I ask for wisdom and I ask for resources. I ask for courage and I ask for holiness. I ask for forgiveness and I ask for blessing. Sometimes he answers and sometimes he does not—and I keep on asking until the answer is "No." We are partners, my Father and I. Asking is as sweet as getting; asking creates intimacy.

ENCOUNTERING THE ONE WHO ASKS

Often my Father asks me to become the answer to my own prayers. The tables are turned. I wrestle. I doubt. I ask for a second opinion. And in the end, usually at least, I obey. I make the phone call. I say the hard word in the sermon. I confront the sin. I give the money. I share a part of myself in a book even when I would rather keep my wounds well hidden. Obeying also creates sweetness. Abraham felt the closeness as he quietly walked Isaac up the rugged slopes of Mount Moriah. Daniel felt the closeness when he chose prayer over life. Matthew felt the closeness when he walked away from his tax practice and cast his lot with the mysterious Rabbi from Galilee. Martin Luther King Jr. felt the closeness when he wrote his letters from the Birmingham jail. Dietrich Bonhoeffer felt the closeness when he preached his last sermon in the Flossenbürg prison camp an hour before the Nazis hanged him. Barbara Youderian felt the closeness when she heard that her husband Roger had been martyred while trying to evangelize the Auca Indians. She wrote in her diary that night in 1956,

> Tonight the Captain told us of his finding four bodies in the river. One had a tee-shirt and blue-jeans. Roj was the only one who wore them. . . . God gave me this verse two days ago, Psalm 48:14, "For this God is our God for ever and ever; He will be our guide even unto death." As I came face to face with the news of Roj's death, my heart was filled with praise. He was worthy of his homegoing. Help me Lord, to be both mummy and daddy.[7]

Being asked, and saying yes, is intimacy.

A friend called me in tears last Sunday afternoon. She had been asking her Father for guidance and suddenly was thrust into the presence of the One Who Asks. He had asked her to live in a land far, far away and tell the people there about Jesus. It was not the first time the Asker had spoken so. She knows that the day of decision is drawing closer. "I am so afraid," she whispered. "So afraid."

I know my friend. She will wrestle. She will cry. She will doubt. But in the end, she will say yes to the One Who Asks. She will lose much. She will gain much more.

The Jeb Stuart Project

We began our church at the height of the church growth movement. For those of you who do not remember it, the church growth movement applied basic principles of sociology to churches in order to help them grow. I learned a lot from church growth teachers and am thankful for their contribution to the kingdom. A popular church growth topic in the eighties was "breaking growth barriers." Researchers discovered that certain churches hit growth plateaus and others keep growing. They became students of the growing churches and tried to find out why they were able to keep growing. Fuller Seminary led the way and offered a series of seminars on "Breaking the 200 Barrier," "Breaking the 400 Barrier," and so on.

When we began hitting 700 in our Sunday morning attendance we seemed to "hit a wall." We were struggling to go to the next level of growth. We decided to take our staff to a Beyond 800 church growth conference to learn the principles that would help us break through the 800-member barrier and keep growing. We piled into the van one Sunday after church and arrived at the Baltimore Holiday Inn late that night.

I arose early the next morning, found a cup of coffee, and headed outside for a prayer walk. When I returned, eager to pick up my conference notebook, I detected a curious lack of standard conference features—like registration tables, signs, and most importantly, other people! Our staff had gathered by now and together we went to the information desk.

"We're here for the Beyond 800 church growth conference," I said.

Then the clerk said the words I dreaded hearing: "What's that?" she asked.

The conference had been canceled. No one had bothered to tell us, and I had not bothered to confirm our registration. We were ten hours away from home on a Monday morning with two days blocked out. What should we do? Tim, our youth pastor, lobbied for a tour of the nearby Harley-Davidson plant, but was quickly vetoed. We decided to drive to Gettysburg, Pennsylvania, and spend the day exploring one of the Civil War's greatest battlefields.

Our Gettysburg tour turned out to be the best church growth conference we have ever attended. We spent the day wandering the freshly mown fields, learning the story of one of the Civil War's most epic battles. When we finally piled back into the van for the long drive home, our minds were filled with vivid images of heroism and horror—of Longstreet and Lee arguing behind a tree line, of Chamberlain's classic stand, of brave men in gray and blue marching to their deaths for a cause they believed deeply in but rarely could articulate.

Jeb Stuart captured our imagination more than any soldier we learned about that day. Jeb Stuart was the flamboyant cavalry officer who had a liking for the ladies and a flair for making headlines. Lee relied heavily on Stuart for information about the enemy's tactics and troop positions. Stuart would ride stealthily behind enemy lines, learn what he needed, and then sprint back to Lee's tent with his report. Once he had grabbed many front-page headlines by circling the northern army without them knowing it. At Gettysburg, he thought he would try the stunt again. When Stuart finally arrived back in camp on the second night of the battle, it was already too late. Lee had been forced to make battle plans without knowing the strength or location of his enemy and sent hundreds of men to their deaths in what became known as Pickett's Charge—one of the Confederate army's greatest losses and a turning point in the war. The fighting on the first two days of the battle had taken place on the left and right flanks. Lee, without Stuart's reconnaissance information, had to guess that the North had flooded all their troops to the right and left flanks, leaving the middle open to attack. He was wrong. General Buford had amassed regiments of his strongest troops during the night behind the hill where Picket would soon lead his fateful charge.

Students of the Battle of Gettysburg blame the South's loss on many factors. Jeb Stuart's failure to protect his troops was certainly one of them.

When we drove home that night it occurred to us that God might want to teach us something through what we had just seen. "We came up here to learn strategies to help us grow," Tim prayed. "We thought we'd learn those strategies at a church growth conference. But you had other plans. What do you want to say to us?"

Mike, who is now our missions pastor and is an avid student of military strategy, immediately knew the answer.

"It's Jeb Stuart," he said. "He was the eyes of the Confederate Army. They had troops and plans, but they didn't have the eyes to see how to make the right plans."

"A lot of men died as a result," Tim added.

"God is talking to us about prayer, guys," Mike went on, his voice becoming more excited. "Prayer shows us how we are to engage the enemy. We are like the Confederates. We have troops and plans, but don't have God's strategy for moving ahead."

We decided that we had to learn how to become a praying church. Church growth principles were good, but not enough to fully engage the enemy. We had to have God's plans. We had to see the future through *his* eyes.

That was the last church growth conference we ever attended. But it was just the beginning of our journey toward becoming a praying church. We came home and began asking God for a prayer strategy. We called our new journey in prayer the Jeb Stuart Project.

The only premise I do not like in the church growth literature is the assumption that if you follow certain growth principles your church will inevitably grow. It simply is not true. Obeying these principles helps. But true spiritual growth is fundamentally a work of the Spirit. Wise strategies and plans, when they are not birthed in prayer, do not win spiritual wars. We accomplish nothing except through prayer.

I am a relatively sharp guy; I know how to make things happen. But I have made too many things happen that God did not want to happen and have seen too many people hurt in the process. That is why I pray a lot more than I used to. I have led too many of my own Picket's Charges into an enemy I did not know was there. I have left too many valiant soldiers lying in their own blood on the battlefield because I made decisions without the eyes of prayer.

A prayer movement is growing in our town. Over a hundred pastors are involved. We are becoming people of prayer for the same reason: impotence. We are tired of running programs and shuffling one another's sheep around while lost people stay lost, and hurt people stay hurt. We worked hard and long and became tired—and the programs remained the same. So now we are praying. Because nothing gets done without prayer.

BROKENNESS AND PRAYER

Brokenness is one of the secrets of prayer.

Praying well is the privilege of people who have been broken, who have come to the end of their own resources, who have tried it all and given their best shot and watched it slip through their fingers anyway. And it is in these broken places—these tired, worn out, frustrated, "I give up" places—that we encounter the sweetness of Jesus.

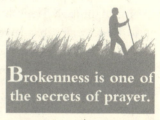

Brokenness is one of the secrets of prayer.

I flipped through some old files recently, pulling out some letters I wrote at the beginning of my ministry. I like the young man who wrote those letters. He is confident, even brash, eager to take the hill, resolute in his drive, fearful of little, convinced of the inevitability of his mission's success.

I miss that young man, but I am not that man anymore. I have been broken. I am scarred. I walk with a limp. Yet I am more of a warrior now than when I was twenty-five. I believe the devil fears me more now than he did when I was twenty-five. Because now I know the impotence of my own strength. And now I am a man of prayer. Prayer has become my strength.

In an article titled "Healing the Tear in the Masculine Soul," Ted Dobson writes:

> There is a "tear" in the masculine soul—a gaping hole or wound that leads to profound insecurity. The German psychologist, Alexander Mitscherlish, has written that society has torn the soul of the male, and into this tear demons have fled—

demons of insecurity, selfishness, and despair. Consequently, men do not know who they are as men. Rather, they define themselves by what they do, who they know, or what they own.[8]

Prayer has helped knit together this tear in my own soul, driving out the demons that have sought refuge there. As I have released my insecurities and fears to my Father, he has replaced them with *his* courage and strength.

PRAYER WITH OTHERS

I have believed in prayer since I was a young Christian. I became committed to prayer after our trip to Gettysburg. I began to love prayer when I began to pray with friends. Friendship with Christ in prayer is often enhanced through friendship with others. I enjoy a night of prayer with close friends more than anything. Sandi and I often pray with loved ones until one or two in the morning. But it has not always been that way.

One Sunday evening about a year into the Jeb Stuart Project, Sandi and I were eating dinner with our next-door neighbors Gary and Debbie. We settled down with dessert in their living room when Gary asked, "Why don't we pray a bit?"

We had spent a lot of evenings together, but prayer was not usually on the agenda. Yet something had changed since we began asking God to make us a praying church. A grassroots prayer movement was beginning to emerge in our congregation. Dr. Paul Cedar, then president of our denomination, was sending monthly letters to all of the Evangelical Free Church pastors challenging us to prayer. He had invited us to begin fasting one day a week, and I had just accepted the challenge. We had read Andrew Murray's *Ministry of Intercession* as a staff team, listened together to Peter Wagner's seminar on prayer, and worked our way through *Rees Howells, Intercessor*. Henry Blackaby's tremendous study *Experiencing God* had made a major impact on our church, stirring hunger to seek God in prayer. And Neal Anderson's Freedom in Christ Ministries had introduced us to the incredible power of praying for someone as they affirm Scripture and renounce sin. The tides of prayer were rising.

We began praying together that night and didn't stop until after midnight. We met again nearly every Sunday night for over a year. And now I love to pray. Our agenda was simple. We did not know how to pray and wanted to learn. We would begin each evening with a simple prayer: "Lord, this is your night. We leave our agendas at the door. Teach us to pray." And he did.

At first we prayed together like a freshman football team. We dropped lots of balls and missed plenty of signals. But the longer we prayed, the more we learned to pray well together. We learned how to discern his prayer agenda for the evening. We truly came in with no agenda other than seeking him. Some nights we would pray for our children. Some nights we would pray for our church. Some nights we would pray for a nation. And some nights we would pray for one another. No night was the same and every night was rich. We found that God usually had one item he wanted us to pray through each night. When we "hit it" we stayed with the theme until we had prayed it through. The more we prayed together the more we learned to appreciate our different prayer styles and strengths. We learned to take what the last person prayed and pray it further.

My memories of that year in "prayer school" are among the richest of my life. It was a safe place, where we checked our Glittering Images at the door and let one another see the darker corners of our nature. We prayed through our failures and our fears, our hopes and our dreams. We prayed through the death of Gary's sister, the birth of our daughter, and the discovery of Bryden's cancer. The dance of prayer became the dance of our lives.

Gary and Debbie's living room was also a place of expectancy. We never knew what God wanted to do on a given night, but we were never disappointed. I remember looking forward to those evenings like a young lover anticipates an evening with his beloved. God never came early. We joked that the Holy Spirit never showed up until eleven o'clock. It did seem to take several hours of catching up, eating, and laughing before our hearts were ready to truly seek him. But that was fine with me. I will take white-hot prayer over sleep any day.

We learned, too, to give the gift of our need to one another and receive prayer. This has never been easy for me, as a pastor. Pastors learn how to share prayer requests, but only heroic ones: "Please pray for me this week as I attempt to save the world." I had felt selfish and exposed when I shared my personal prayer needs with others.

Not anymore. Some of my most intimate moments with my Savior occur when my brothers and sisters lay hands on me and pray. Their hands become the hands of Jesus. Today a team of twenty people prays for me five days a week. I email them several times each week with specific prayer requests. A prayer team joins me for the first two hours of my sermon preparation on Thursdays. Another team prays through each Sunday service; I email them my sermon notes in advance. A prayer team has been in the cabin with me in an adjacent room during the writing of this book, praying for both me and you. I took two members of my prayer team with me when I went to Vanderbilt Voice Center recently for help with my strained vocal chords. They prayed for me in the car on the drive to Nashville, prayed with me in the waiting room, prayed with me during my exam, and prayed with me on the way home.

"Pray also for me," Paul wrote the Ephesians.[9] I have voiced the same request many, many times. Prayer has become one of the most intimate parts of my spiritual life. The people I pray with are the people I am closest with. And the closer I am with them, the closer I am with my Father.

PRAYING ALONE

Earlier in my Christian life, before I learned to pray, I dreaded being alone. I remember in college making plans on Tuesday for dinner on Saturday because I could not bear the thought of eating alone. My prayer life struggled because, I told myself, I was simply too busy. I was too busy. But I had a motive for my busyness: I feared being alone.

Many people I know abhor the deafening silence of solitude. I once gave a man I was counseling an assignment: spend a half a day alone.

"No books," I said. "No TV. No radio. Just your Bible, a journal, and a pen."

Beads of sweat appeared on his forehead. Fear was in his eyes. "I can't do that," he said. We never met again.

I feared being alone because in solitude the tear in my soul was exposed. I knew who I was with others, and I lost that person when I was alone.

Dr. Ashworth, whom we met a few pages ago, never faced the tear in his own soul until he was forced to spend a season alone in the monastery. The first moments of solitude nearly destroyed him. Father Darrow guides him through.

> I gasped, "I'm cut off from God." I was in terror. I was shuddering from head to foot. Tears were streaming down my face. "He's gone. He's rejected me. He's not here—"
>
> "He's here but you can't see him. You've been blinded..."
>
> "I'm being invaded." I was shuddering again, gasping for breath. "Without God—all the demons—taking over—telling me I'm not fit to—"
>
> "Take this." He shoved his pectoral cross hard into my hand. "The cross bars their path. No demon can withstand the power of Christ.... Now I'm going to say a prayer for you, a silent prayer, and I want you to listen with your mind and try to hear what I'm saying."
>
> Silence fell. I obediently listened but heard nothing. However, after a while I became aware in my darkness of a strange heat.... I opened my eyes to find he was watching me, and as our glances met, he said: "Did you hear the prayer?"
>
> "No, but I remember Our Lord saying: 'Lo, I am with you always, even unto the end of the world.'"[10]

Ashworth discovered that his faith was a Glittering Image as well, a cultivated external shell with little internal reality. When he was alone, the demons rushed to fill his soul. Prayer drove them away.

The same has happened in my life. Shortly after the Jeb Stuart Project began, I began to spend a day alone each week in prayer, fasting, and the study of Scripture. This proved to be one of the most difficult choices I have ever made. It meant phone messages would go unanswered, hospital visits would not be made, and lunch appointments would have to wait for another day. Beneath these legitimate pastoral reasons was a lurking fear of what I might find when I spent the day with a stranger—my isolated self. But I made the choice. I have met Christ in the lonely places. And he has driven many of the demons away.

Now my day alone is the anchor of my week. Fasting cleanses my mind and intensifies my soul's hunger for God. Gazing at the sleepy waters of the Tennessee, ambling lazily beneath rocky banks shaded with maple trees and dogwoods, slows the pace of my inner world.

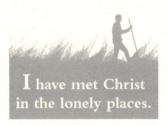

I have met Christ in the lonely places.

I begin the day by journaling. This helps me center into the parts of my heart that are inaccessible to me in normal hours. I try to be as honest as I can be about what I need and what I want, how I have sinned and where I need direction. I spend much of the day in the Word, studying and meditating on the text I am to preach on Sunday. The final hours are spent walking.

I love to walk with the Lord. The Word, dwelling richly within me, begins to intersect with the heart issues surfaced in my journaling. My body, empty now of food and longing for it, is especially sensitive to the Lord's whispers. When five o'clock comes, I am eager to eat, but sorry to leave the One I love. Sometimes I sit a few moments longer, soaking in these rare, precious moments of prayerful intimacy.

When I travel, I love to find quiet places to walk with the Lord. Many of my fondest memories with him are from walks we have taken together. These memories flood my mind: a rainy walk to Dawson Trotman's grave site in the mountains above Glen Eyrie, Colorado; a moonlight walk on the beach on Harbor Island, Bahamas; a sober walk through a Buddhist graveyard in Dalatt, Vietnam; a chilly walk through the Romanian alps; a thoughtful walk along the paths of Blackberry Farm.

In my quiet walks, I share my heart with Jesus. And he shares his heart with me.

Charles Ashworth, as Darrow gently leads him toward the mysteries of his heart, observes, "I felt my Glittering Image begin to slip."

This is the work of prayer.

SEVEN

SHARED INTIMACIES

God gave me the gift of prayer language at a time in my spiritual journey when I was desperate to turn my knowledge of propositions *about* God into personal knowledge *of* God. We were studying Romans 5–8 as a congregation. The deeper we went into this classic description of life in Christ, the more troubled I became. Paul seemed to be describing an intimate, experiential friendship with Christ that I knew little of. Chapter 5 reminded me that "God has poured out his love into our hearts by the Holy Spirit."[1] I remember enthusiastically preaching that the word "poured out" was the word we get "cascade" from. "We should experience God's love pouring over us like a waterfall," I thundered. But that was not my experience.

Chapter 6 promised me that I had been united with Christ in his resurrection. This has always been one of my favorite metaphors for life in Christ. Yet it was still just a metaphor, an idea, not a reality in my experience.

Chapter 7 begins by comparing our relationship with Christ to a marriage union. And chapter 8? Well, chapter 8 about did me in. Paul describes the spiritual life as a life "led by the spirit," a life so intimately connected to Christ that I could "cry Abba Father" and hear the Spirit's voice testifying to me that I am indeed God's child.[2] We spent two years in these four chapters. One afternoon in the middle of this series, I took a walk through the woods and cried out, "God, I believe your Word. I believe that what Paul is describing is what you want for every believer. Yet this is so far from what I know. Please, let what I preach become what I live!" I kept taking those walks and continued praying those prayers.

One morning toward the end of our time in Romans I was on my knees fasting and praying in a little mountain cabin. My frustrated longing to live out what I was preaching week after week in Romans had only intensified. "Dear Jesus," I prayed. "I want to know you. I want to experience the kind of Christianity Paul describes in Romans. I don't just want to know about you! I want to know you!"

Suddenly, a river of words from a language I did not know welled up within me and burst from my mouth in a flash flood of prayer and praise. I lay on the floor worshiping and praying for what must have been two hours before the river subsided. God had given me the gift of spiritual language.

I wish I could tell you that my new prayer language revolutionized my spiritual life and immediately transformed me into a radically improved Christian. It did not. But my prayer language did help me experience the living God. His living Spirit was praying through me. Somehow God did not seem as remote anymore. His Holy Spirit was present, praying through me.

The German theologian Rudolf Otto, in his classic work *The Idea of the Holy,* wrote that while true religion begins with a rational knowing of God, it must never end there. He says the heart of true religion is an emotional response to God, which he calls "mysterium tremendum." The worshiper, in encountering God, feels "mystical awe" and a "feeling of personal nothingness and submergence before the awe-inspiring object directly experienced."[3] I touch the mysterium tremendum when I pray in my spiritual language. This gift helps a man who lives out of his head begin the slow journey toward a heartfelt faith.

Paul says that when we pray this way we speak mysteries to God. Mysteries, in biblical usage, are secrets that are now revealed. When I pray in my spiritual language, secret chambers in my heart are unlocked; chambers that I simply cannot open with the key of my mind.

Jesus and Paul on Spiritual Language

Paul practiced two kinds of praying.[4] "I will pray with my spirit," he says. "I will also pray with my mind." Praying with the mind, obviously, is the kind of prayer we described in the last chapter. But what is praying with the spirit? Paul calls this kind of prayer "speaking in tongues."[5]

Paul says, "Anyone who speaks in a tongue does not speak to men but to God. . . . He utters mysteries with his spirit."[6] When we pray in tongues we are praying "mysteries" to God; we are using spiritual words our mind does not understand. Since the word "tongue" literally means "language," many today describe praying in tongues as praying with their spiritual language, or praying with their prayer language. A prayer language is a spiritual gift, given by the Holy Spirit to some believers to help them pray.[7] When a person receives a prayer language, they have received the ability to pray in a spiritual language. Paul is very fond of praying with spiritual language. Listen to what he says about this spiritual gift:

> If you praise him in the private prayer language of tongues . . .
> you are sharing intimacies just between you and him.[8]
> The one who prays using a private "prayer language" certainly
> gets a lot out of it.[9]
> I would like every one of you to speak in tongues.[10]
> I'm grateful to God for the gift of praying in tongues that he gives
> us for praising him, which leads to wonderful intimacies we enjoy
> with him.[11]
> Do not forbid speaking in tongues.[12]

The New Testament does not talk a great deal about the personal spirituality of first century believers. We find a clue that many early believers may have had the gift of spiritual language from the final verses of Mark's gospel, where Jesus says that his followers will "speak with new tongues."[13] Many scholars do not believe the final verses of Mark's gospel were in the original manuscripts. Most believe these verses were added by the church in the early second century. This could mean that a century after Christ's death and resurrection, the early church thought praying with a spiritual language

When we pray in tongues we are praying "mysteries" to God.

was a normal part of personal spirituality. According to New Testament scholar Gordon Fee, "it was the common, everyday experience of the early church to pray in this manner."[14]

TOUCHING A WIDOW'S HEART

Praying in spiritual language is becoming a common, everyday experience for many of the people I walk through life with. Just as husbands and wives do not share the intimacies of the bedroom with others, most people I know do not talk much about their experience with spiritual language—it is too private. When they do talk, it is usually because I have asked them to help me understand this gift better so I can explain it to others. I find a refreshing balance in the way the people in our church approach this gift. Spiritual language is seen as simply one of many gifts the Spirit gives to help us serve and know the Son.

Della, a member of our staff team, received the gift of spiritual language several months after losing her husband Dick to cancer. "Can I share something with you?" Della asked one morning as I passed her desk on the way to my office. We caught up on how she was handling Dick's death. The months following the funeral had been barren and frightening. "After Dick died, I wanted to die," Della quietly shared. "Nothing had meaning. I had no reason to go on." Della's dark grief gradually turned into a desperate longing for God. "I began to feel a hunger for God that just grew and grew," she remembers. "I'd never felt anything like it."

One afternoon the hunger grew so intense that Della drove to a friend's house and asked her to pray. Her friend asked her what she wanted. "I want as much of God as he'll let me have," she answered, and closed her eyes as her friend prayed. "I began praising the Lord, first in English, and then, little by little, with new words. Later that night, the words just flowed out."

Della's spiritual language has played a significant role in helping her overcome her grief over Dick's death. "Praying this way has helped fill the empty hole I had after Dick was gone," Della explains. "God is my husband now. My prayer language has helped me become much more intimate with him."

Spiritual Language and Releasing Emotions

Spiritual language also helps us release emotions in prayer that are buried deep within us. Paul promised that "the Spirit helps us in our weakness. We do not know what we ought to pray for, but the Spirit himself intercedes for us with groans that words cannot express."[15] Scholars disagree on whether or not Paul was talking about spiritual language in this verse. Certainly all prayer is aided by the Spirit. We can be confident that the Spirit is eager to help anyone who seeks his aid in prayer, regardless of whether or not they have the gift of spiritual language.

If Romans 8:26-27 does not refer exclusively to praying with spiritual language, it certainly *includes* this kind of prayer. I have found that spiritual language helps us release parts of our inner world to God in prayer that are difficult to draw out in English.

Richard asked Sandi and I to pray for him one night because he was chronically fatigued and depressed. "I don't know what's wrong with me," he said. "I've been to counseling. I know what my issues are. I just can't seem to break free of this."

After a time of worship, we asked the Holy Spirit to show us any wound in Richard's soul that had healed improperly, allowing spiritual infection to settle in. "I'm with my father," Richard whispered, describing the memory now fresh in his mind. "He's dying. He's still alive physically, but he's gone."

"How do you feel, Richard?"

"I don't know. I don't feel anything, really."

As we asked the Holy Spirit to help Richard experience appropriate emotions, Richard began to weep.

"What do you feel now?"

"I feel like screaming. I'm so angry. I need him. I am the youngest. He is the only one who understands me." The memory pressed in upon Richard, and time collapsed. "Dad! Dad! Don't go. Don't go. Who will be there for me? Who will help me? You can't! You can't!"

A river of anger was swirling within Richard, a river that needed to be released and replaced with the healing waters of the Spirit. Yet this memory had been buried so long that Richard could not fully release them.

"Richard, you have a prayer language don't you? Why don't you just begin to pray? The Spirit will help you release what you need to in prayer."

Reluctantly, Richard began to pray in his spiritual language. The words came haltingly at first, and then, as if a dam broke somewhere within him, a torrent of words flowed out, carrying with them twenty years of pent-up anger and pain. Several minutes later, the wound had been fully cleansed, and we invited Christ to heal this painful memory in Richard's life.

Later, I asked Richard what he was experiencing as he released his emotions through spiritual language. "I'd buried those feelings deep inside me. I didn't even know they were there. When I began to pray, all kinds of emotions surged to the surface. It was like the Holy Spirit was cleaning out everything, releasing all the junk that was in there."

A CRY FOR HEALING

Many times those who desire spiritual language are really crying out for inner healing similar to the kind Richard experienced. I am learning not to pray for someone to receive this gift as soon as they ask for it. Instead, I ask the Holy Spirit to first reveal if anything is hindering intimacy in the person's life.

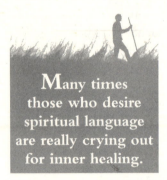

Many times those who desire spiritual language are really crying out for inner healing.

Ellen asked several of us to pray for her. She had been seeking the gift of spiritual language for some time and was wondering why God had not answered her prayers. I explained to her that the goal of our prayer time was simply to seek whatever the Lord wanted for her and leave the matter of gifts up to him. She agreed, and we began to ask the Holy Spirit to lead our prayer time.

"What's going on inside of you, Ellen?" I asked after several moments.

Ellen was quiet for a long time before she spoke. "My husband divorced me ten years ago. I've been terrified of intimacy ever since. I won't give my heart to anyone, even Jesus. It just hurts too much."

Gradually, Ellen began to reveal a deep fear of intimacy that plagued all of her relationships, including her relationship with Christ. We asked Jesus to heal the painful wound left from her divorce, and I began to wrap up the prayer time, thinking we were through. I prayed a final prayer for Ellen, and then, sensing that Ellen was still working through some issues, asked, "Is the Holy Spirit finished yet?"

Ellen looked up and smiled. "He has put a phrase in my mind. Should I pray it?" She did, and began her own journey into the mystery of spiritual language. Ellen's journey, like those of many others, was about a lot more than speaking in tongues.

HELP IN SPIRITUAL BATTLE

Paul says that the Spirit helps us pray when "we do not know what to pray for." Often times during seasons of intense spiritual battle I sense that I need to pray but do not know quite what to pray for. I can discern that evil is afoot but do not know the appropriate prayer response. Spiritual language helps direct my prayers in heavenly battle when I cannot see my enemy. I experience a unique kind of partnering in this kind of intercession that draws me close to the Father's heart.

One evening I was awakened by the Spirit and knew immediately I needed to engage in warfare prayer. I prayed quietly in English at first, slowly waking up, but uncertain who was in need of prayer. As I began to pray in my spiritual language, I had a distinct vision that one of our pastors and his family were being demonically tormented. I sat up in bed and prayed with considerable intensity. Waves of nausea and a palpable heaviness came over me. I considered going to the bathroom to vomit, then realized that this was more a consequence of the spiritual warfare than merely a physical problem. After twenty minutes, the sense of danger lessened, and the darkness that I felt in my own bedroom was gone. This pastor told me that he and his wife were in the middle of a discouraging struggle at the time I was led to pray for him.

George Mallone explains, "In spiritual warfare, the language of the mind can only . . . shed little light. Praying in tongues is often a means of battle against this vague and elusive enemy. The Spirit knows what is happening in the battle and through tongues is able to lead in the proper intercession."[16]

Paul warns us that "our struggle is not against flesh and blood, but against the rulers, against the authorities, against the powers of this dark world and against the spiritual forces of evil in the heavenly realms."[17] He then tells us to wage aggressive spiritual warfare against these dark forces by using seven spiritual weapons. He concludes his description of these seven types of weaponry by charging us to "pray in the Spirit on all occasions with all kinds of prayers and requests."[18] Prayer in the Spirit is the seventh weapon of spiritual warfare.

Is Paul really talking about spiritual language here? Again, scholars are divided. Prayer of any kind does tremendous damage to the Enemy. We *can* wage significant warfare in the heavenlies with prayers with the mind. Yet we cannot help but notice that Paul uses the same words here that he uses in 1 Corinthians 14 to describe praying in spiritual language. At the very least, spiritual language is one type of warfare prayer. Could he mean that the gift of spiritual language is a special weapon given to troops for heavenly combat? "If that catches some of us off guard because it is so little a part of the prayer life of most people in the church," notes Gordon Fee, "we probably ought not to read our experience of church back into the life of Paul."[19]

Recently a team from our church traveled to Romania to serve a team of American missionaries. We arrived a day early and drove to the conference site so we could rest, pray, and prepare. As I worked on my talks in my hotel room, my spirit grew restless; I sensed trouble afoot. Setting aside my notes and grabbing my coat, I headed outside for a prayer walk. I prayed through several scriptural promises, but felt like I needed to pray more. I just did not know how to pray. I began to pray quietly in my prayer language and continued to circle the hotel where the conference was going to be held. An image came to my mind of a large black panther with angry yellow eyes stalking the hotel site. I sensed this panther represented demonic forces arrayed against the missionaries. Then a series of bars appeared before the panther, keeping it from attacking.

Reflecting on this image, I sensed that God was saying that the bars represented prayers and that fervent prayer would protect us from spiritual attack. The rest of our team affirmed this, and added that they too were sensing intense heavenly conflict. We emailed our prayer team back in the States, who immediately began to pray. We awoke the next morning and began the conference with a sense that the danger had passed and with Paul's warning that "our struggle is not against flesh and blood, but against . . . the spiritual forces of evil in the heavenly realms" very much on our minds. God had used the gift of spiritual language to protect us from spiritual danger.

SPIRITUAL LANGUAGE AND THE PROPHETIC

Most of the uses of spiritual language we have been discussing deal with our personal, private prayer life. This seems to be the primary place where this gift is used. Yet spiritual language can serve in a prophetic sense in gatherings of believers when God also gives the gift of interpretation.[20] We can be touched by God's intimate, personal care for the details of our lives as God intersects our world through a prophetic message in tongues. Speaking of this setting, Paul says, "anyone who speaks in a tongue should pray that he may interpret what he says."[21] Uninterpreted spiritual language is not permitted in the corporate worship service because words that cannot be understood do not build up the body. Spiritual language with interpretation, however, does.[22]

Sometimes the interpretation is a line-by-line, word-by-word translation. Most of the time, however, the interpretation simply gives the sense of the meaning. Linguists call this "holophrastic" communication. Holophrastic language occurs when a single word may express a complete thought. For example, when a small child says "ball" her parents know that she means, "I want the red ball in the corner."[23] A similar process apparently takes place when a word given in spiritual language is interpreted. The interpretation may not be precisely parallel in length to the word given in tongues.

Jackie Pullinger tells of the remarkable, encouraging prophetic ministry of interpreted prayer language in her biography *Chasing the Dragon,* a gripping autobiography about ministry to young people in Hong Kong's infamous Forbidden City. "As we were praying I had a message in tongues and one of the boys interpreted immediately. . . . He could not read the

Bible and he had only believed in Jesus a few days before this event," she writes. "But his interpretation was a clear, direct quotation from Psalms 126 and 127. These spiritual babes through the working of the Holy Spirit were able to say exactly the right words to me at that time."[24]

Before I left for my writing sabbatical I asked several friends to pray for me. I shared with them that I was looking forward to the extended time writing, but was anxious about my ability to put into words what God had put in my heart. One of them prayed in a spiritual language over me. Then God granted another the interpretation: "I have anointed your hands to write." Those words have ministered to me again and again during these long days of writing. They have fulfilled the purpose of prophecy—strengthening, comforting, and encouraging my heart.

SPIRITUAL LANGUAGE AND WORSHIP

Spiritual language also provides us with a new way of expressing worship to God. "I will sing with my spirit," Paul says, adding, "I will also sing with my mind."[25] Singing with the Spirit is similar to praying with the Spirit. Not only can we pray with our spiritual language, we can also praise with this gift. The same rules for corporate worship apply, so we assume that the natural expression for singing in the Spirit is in one's personal prayer life. Perhaps this is one way we can follow Paul's instruction to "sing psalms, hymns and spiritual songs with gratitude in your hearts to God."[26] Every worship song is a spiritual song. Yet so are the songs the Spirit sings through us when we praise God with our spiritual language.

I am musically challenged and cannot read music or remember lyrics very well. It is difficult for me to sing praise songs or hymns when I am alone because often I do not remember the words. I can, though, "sing in the Spirit." I simply begin to sing in my spiritual language. A melody emerges, the notes gently gliding up and down the scale like a carefree butterfly flitting over a summer meadow. Remarkably, this is as close as I ever get to singing on key!

THE HEALING POWER OF SPIRITUAL WORDS

Language is alive with spiritual power. When Isaac released the words of blessing upon Jacob, he could not call them back, no matter how much he longed to bless Esau with them. They had escaped his lips and now had a life of their own. Words of blessing and words of cursing in the Bible were matters of immense consequence: the words of a blessing changed your life forever, the words of a curse could do the same. Words are "vehicles of supernatural, spiritual power," writes Derek Prince.[27]

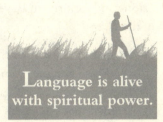

Language is alive with spiritual power.

This is equally true with the words of spiritual language. Significant spiritual power is released when we pray over someone with our spiritual language. Such prayers can release a life-giving river of spiritual words that refresh and cleanse a weary soul.

The question is often asked, "But doesn't spiritual language need interpretation when done in public?" To answer this, we need to remember Paul's purpose in writing 1 Corinthians. The setting is a public worship service. He does not want someone standing up and speaking in a spiritual language nobody can understand because the worship service is a place for intelligibility. He is also concerned with being "seeker sensitive" and does not want a non-believing guest to come in and say, "You are out of your mind."[28]

It is not hard to see why uninterpreted spiritual language in the worship service is forbidden. The setting I am describing, though, is much different. I am thinking of sitting in my living room with a friend, or lying on the bed with one of my children, or praying on the couch with my wife. These are entirely different settings than the one Paul is speaking about in 1 Corinthians 14. In some of these settings the Spirit may lead us to intercede for a friend in our spiritual language. Interpretation is not necessary. The Spirit has no desire to speak to our minds; he simply wants to pray through us over one of his own weary sheep, to "intercede for us with groans that words cannot express." I find great refreshment in this ministry of prayer, especially during times of weariness and discouragement. When a friend prays, I can sense spiritual power washing over me, restoring me, watering my dry and thirsty soul.

Finding words to describe the ministry of the Holy Spirit in this way has been difficult. One evening I was reading Tolkien's *The Fellowship of the Ring* to my children when I came across a passage that comes as close as anything I have ever read to what it is like to be ministered to by someone praying over you in their spiritual language. Frodo is resting "alone and forlorn" in Rivendell, when he hears the beautiful language of the elves.

> At first the beauty of the melodies of the interwoven words in the Elven-tongue, even though he understood them little, held him in a spell, as soon as he began to attend to them. Almost it seemed that the words took shape, and visions of far lands and bright things that he had never yet imagined opened out before him; and the firelit hall became like a golden mist above seas of foam that sighed upon the margins of the world. Then the enchantment became more and more dreamlike, until he felt that an endless river of swelling gold and silver was flowing over him, too multitudinous for its pattern to be comprehended; it became part of the throbbing air about him, and it drenched and drowned him. Swiftly, he sank under its shining weight into a deep realm of sleep.[29]

Tolkien's richly woven description is an experience that resonates with my own.

SHOULD WE SEEK THE GIFT OF SPIRITUAL LANGUAGE?

We find a tension in Scripture as we look for an answer to this question. On the one hand Paul asks, "All do not speak with tongues, do they?"[30] The answer he clearly expects is, "No." The entire point of 1 Corinthians 12 is that there are many different gifts in the body of Christ, sovereignly distributed by a wise and loving Spirit. We should not expect each of us to have the same gift.

On the other hand, Paul also says, "I would like every one of you to speak in tongues."[31]

How do we resolve this tension? I believe that if you do not want the gift of spiritual language you probably will not receive it. If you do desire this gift, you probably will. I believe the Holy Spirit puts a desire for this gift on the hearts of some and not on the hearts of others. We must give others the freedom to not want this gift! We do not have to all pray the same way. This is the beauty of the diversity in the body of Christ. Christians who simply do not have any desire for this gift should not feel condemned or judged. Bible study and prayer are biblical commands. Speaking in tongues is not.

What should you do if you desire a spiritual language? Let's begin by remembering what we are not saying. We are *not* saying that spiritual language is the essential evidence of being filled with the Spirit. We are *not* saying that spiritual language will revolutionize your life. We are *definitely not* saying that a believer cannot have a vital, powerful prayer life without this gift. We are saying that spiritual language is one of a number of spiritual disciplines that has helped many nurture their love relationship with Jesus.

The Holy Spirit is uniquely creative in how he works with his children. Any attempt to make normative the Spirit's work ("he always works like this") is a hot tip that you are headed for trouble. The Spirit is sovereign! He gives spiritual gifts "just as he determines."[32] Some receive a prayer language in private—as I did. Others receive their language while others pray for them. I have even known believers who have woken up in the middle of the night praying in their new language.

A discernable pattern, though, does commonly occur when we receive the gift of spiritual language.

Ask

We begin by asking. Many times someone who has learned about this gift will say, "Well, I'm open. God can give me anything he wants. I won't stop him." Yet Paul, in the opening words of an entire chapter about spiritual language, urges, "eagerly desire spiritual gifts."[33] We must begin by asking. Seeking and asking almost always precedes spiritual blessing.

Speak

Most people have to take a step of faith when they receive their prayer language. Begin speaking by faith, trusting God to fill your mouth with new words. Often God will give you one word or a short phrase.

You are only responsible for speaking the phrase out. This is the beginning of a new vocabulary for you. Like a child, you are just learning a new language. You may pray this phrase for weeks until the Holy Spirit expands your vocabulary.

Other times God will give a steady flow of words at the very beginning. Either way, you cannot sit there passively and expect God to move you. He always invites us to join him in faith in what he is doing.

Relax

Should you not receive the gift, relax. Do not try forcing it. And certainly do not believe the lie that God must not love you because he did not immediately answer your prayer. He often delays answering our prayers for reasons only known to him. Should this remain a desire of your heart, persevere.

Practice

Spiritual language, like normal language, needs constant practice to be developed. I spent two years studying Greek in seminary but have not studied Greek since. Now I have forgotten most of it. You cannot grow in a language without frequently using it. Often people will receive a spiritual language, stop using it for years, and then disparage the gift, dismissing its value with a polite, "It didn't really do much for me." No language is useful if we never use it. Spiritual language is no different. It must be cultivated with frequent use if it is to grow.

SHARING OUR HEARTS WITH OUR BELOVED

We pray with our mind. And we pray with our spirit.

George Buttrick had it right when he said that prayer is friendship. We nurture our friendship with our beloved friend by hearing his heart for us and sharing our heart with him. Paul tells us how to nurture our relationship with God: prayer. We pray with our mind. And we pray with our spirit.

EIGHT

THE FELLOWSHIP OF HIS SUFFERINGS

A counselor friend and I once roomed together at a conference. He is a very wise man and has earned a reputation as one of our city's best marriage counselors. We talked long after the lights went out, ruining any hope of staying awake during the lectures the next day.

"What's the single most devastating problem you see in marriages?" I asked my sleepy friend, trying to squeeze just a few more insights from him before he drifted off to sleep.

"Disappointment," he said, without even a pause to think about it. "We don't know what to do when we become disappointed with our spouse." Every marriage that goes the distance eventually must cope with disappointment. We, after all, are fallen, flawed people. And no one knows that better than our spouse.

Sandi loves me deeply. I sense that she is truly *for* me. She believes in me. She delights in the parts of me that bring God glory. She makes personal sacrifices so that I can fulfill God's calling on my life. She is proud of me.

Yet she is also disappointed. As we draw near the close of our second decade of marriage, she can see the fine print on the contract. She knows she has married a man that sometimes loves his ministry more than his family; who expresses his thoughts and feelings more eloquently from a pulpit than he can over a candlelit dinner; who continually loses his keys, wallet, day timer, and even an occasional kid in a crowded mall; and who could not hang wallpaper straight if his life depended on it.

Scratch long enough to go beneath the surface of any marriage, and you will find disappointment. What we do with that disappointment determines the long-term health of our marriage. Many allow the collective disappointments of married life to build up, leaving a residue of bitterness and anger coating our souls. Respect is gradually, or suddenly, lost. Trust erodes. Bricks of silence, schedule demands, and cynicism form a wall between former lovers. And intimacy is lost forever.

Mature, healthy, life-giving marriages are not lacking disappointment. Healthy marriages grow out of the hearts of people who have learned how to let their disappointments in one another drive them first to God, then to one another.

Suggesting that we can also become disappointed with Jesus—and that handling disappointment with our eternal Lover is one of the critical tasks of soul shaping—borders on irreverence. After all, Jesus never fails us. Jesus, the perfect Son of God, is never anything less than everything we need him to be.

Yet life is hard. And sometimes we do not believe that Jesus cares when we cry out to him amidst our suffering. The silence of heaven is terrifying, deafening in the fact that we hear nothing at all. The Old Testament prophets were men of great faith who bravely faced their own disappointment with God, hurling hard questions at the heavens and not always getting answers.

> The silence of heaven is terrifying, deafening in the fact that we hear nothing at all.

"Why do you tolerate wrong?" cries Habakkuk.[1] "Why does the way of the wicked prosper?" wonders Jeremiah.[2] King David, whose love for God was only matched by his disappointment in him, shouted to an empty heaven, "How long will the enemy mock you, O God? Will the foe revile your name forever? Why do you hold back your hand?"[3] An ancient biblical poet demands, "Why do you hide your face?"[4]

We know in our heads that God is good and wise and strong. We believe that not even a sparrow falls to the ground without him knowing it. Yet when senseless, irrational chaos breaks loose in our lives, we cannot help but wonder, "Where is God?" Sometimes the gap between personal pain and biblical promise becomes so wide no bridge seems able to cross it.

Philip Yancey wrote the book *Disappointment with God* in response to hundreds of letters he received after writing *Where Is God When It Hurts?* Sometimes the letter-writers told harrowing tales of senseless tragedies that had shaken their faith to the core. But just as often, the person struggling with divine disappointment had more mundane concerns. Yancey found himself in this second category. "I have found that petty disappointments tend to accumulate over time, undermining my faith with a lava flow of doubt," he writes. "I start to wonder whether God cares about everyday details—about me. I am tempted to pray less often, having concluded in advance it won't matter."[5]

Few threats to the spiritual life are more dangerous than disappointment with God. We can awake from these dark nights of the soul to find a wall encircling our hearts: If God will not protect us, we will do it ourselves. Trust deteriorates. Passion ebbs away. Other gods, gods we can touch and taste and feel when we are hurting, catch our eye.

Disappointment with God, however, need not be fatal. One of the grand ironies of our faith is that we can come to know God more intimately by recklessly pursuing him in the dark night of our pain. The prophets, singers, and kings cited above did not settle for existential cynicism; they let their painful questions drive them deeper into the heart of God.

How can disappointment with God help us become more intimate with God instead of less? To answer this we must remember the wisdom of paradox. "Truth," Parker Palmer reminds us, "is found not by splitting the world into either-ors but by embracing it as both-and."[6] Such a paradigm allows us to come to grips with our disappointment with God by freeing us to glean wisdom from both the evangelical and charismatic traditions—even though they each approach the matter of suffering and disappointment very differently. We must listen to each other on this issue more than any. We must put aside the laziness of either-or thinking.

Evangelicals remind us that suffering can in fact be a gift from God, a divine means of helping us enter into a profoundly intimate encounter with Christ that Paul calls "the fellowship of his sufferings." Evangelical literature on the problem of pain is filled with the testimonies of men and women who have come to know their Savior in incredibly rich ways as they have clung to him through the diseases of tragedy and pain.

Charismatics remind us that suffering can also be an attack of Satan and that Jesus accompanied his preaching ministry with many healings. Just as the temple beggar danced and sang when Christ healed him through Peter's prayer, so our hearts are filled with warm feelings of intimate gratitude when Jesus heals us. Charismatic literature abounds with the stories of the healed men and women who have cried out in faith and been delivered from their affliction by a Messiah who still heals today.

"In certain circumstances, truth is a paradoxical joining of apparent opposites," explains Parker Palmer. "If we want to know that truth, we must learn to embrace those opposites as one."[7] This is good advice for us as we embrace two legitimate answers to one of life's most difficult questions: How can I meet God in my suffering? Do I pray for growth as I struggle, or do I pray for deliverance from my struggle?

TWO TRAGEDIES, TWO OUTCOMES

Tim became a Christian in December of 1993. He committed suicide in December of 1996.

Tim gave his heart to Christ after watching his best friend Mark suffer through the death of his baby daughter, Amy. Mark, a brilliant young father of two, finishing up a doctorate in immunology, wrote me this note one year after Amy's funeral.

> Dear Doug,
>
> I cannot minimize the profound sense of despair brought on by Amy's death. My flesh aches when I think of what it would be like to hold her hand or see her in the little Christmas dress that was just a little too large for her to wear last year. . . . Yet in

this loss God has overwhelmed us with His love. . . . During the darkest days, when we were lost in the valley, God lifted us up and carried us beyond it. . . .

As God's words filtered through you that cold, gray December day [the day of Amy's funeral] they touched a young man in attendance named Tim. Tim has been my closest friend for the last eighteen years. . . . Last month he asked Christ into his heart. Saturday we had the opportunity to hike through a snowstorm in the Smokies. It was a splendid day. During the course of our hike we talked in depth of the wonder of God's creation, of his great love for us, of the miracle of Amy's short life and the lessons she had taught us. Tim has a long way to go as far as his understanding of the victory gained by Christ on the cross. But, as he told me on the trail, having experienced God's redemptive power, he can never turn back. God has a great work in store for Tim. Would you keep him in your prayers?

A few months ago Mark sent me a letter informing me of Tim's suicide and explaining some of the story that led up to it. Tim had been touched by the grace of Christ. But a terrible relationship with his family, a painful divorce, financial stress, and shattered self-esteem drove him to despair. Tim desperately tried to cling to God's promises during his three years as a believer—when they found his body his hand was holding a list of Scripture promises Mark had mailed him years before. Yet the ravine between promise and pain stretched ever wider, and Tim eventually plummeted into it. A few hours after signing his divorce papers, Tim cleaned his room and then shot himself in the head with a high-caliber pistol.

Mark included Tim's suicide note in his last letter to me.

Dogs get 3 cups in A.M. *and 3 cups in* P.M. *Lots of biscuits on walks. Change H₂O every 3-4 days. They are good dogs.*

Postlude:

My reasoning behind this choice can be summed up in the following quote: "Life doesn't mean much more than what the thrush said to the snail just before she knocked him on the rock. 'Get up or get out, Lazy Bones.'"

Please know that I made this choice in August and tried to time it for when the divorce was final. Nothing or no one could have deterred me from this goal. I do not defend this choice. I am wrong. . . .

You know if I loved you. Thank you for loving me. I just couldn't love myself.

Those of you who need to . . . Learn from this.

I believe in you.

Two tragedies. Two letters. Two very different outcomes. Both men knew the sting of suffering. Both had prayed to a silent heaven. Both had their own reasons for being disappointed with God. Yet Mark met Jesus in his daughter's death. Tim became entangled in his own despair . . . and lost sight of his Savior.

MEANWHILE, WHERE IS GOD?

Tim is not the first to suffer spiritual sickness because of suffering. "Meanwhile, where is God?" complained C. S. Lewis, whose own faith nearly collapsed in the despair of his own grief after the death of his wife. "Go to him when your need is desperate, when all other help is in vain, and what do you find? A door slammed in your face, and a sound of bolting and double bolting on the inside. After that, silence. You might as well turn away."[8]

Yet Lewis eventually did not turn away, and his story of finding God amidst his suffering has become a classic account of how one man turned disappointment with God into deeper communion with him.

THE FELLOWSHIP OF SHARED SUFFERING

I have experienced two seasons of suffering in my life. Bryden spent nine days in Children's Hospital after surgery that removed a three-pound tumor from her kidney. Tucked away in the basement of the hospital is a small interfaith chapel. God and I had many conversations about suffering in that little chapel. Each time I knelt in the dimly lit room, I found myself drawn to Paul's words in Philippians 3:10: "I want to know Christ and the power of his resurrection and the fellowship of sharing in his sufferings, becoming like him in his death."

Suffering creates a peculiar kind of fellowship with Christ. When we become so broken before him that we have no other place to turn, we gain a closeness, a nearness, an intimate bonding. I touched that closeness in my times in Children's Hospital chapel. The Friday after Bryden was diagnosed I was scheduled to speak at a banquet for our leaders. When I stood to speak that night, I forgot just about everything I was supposed to say. I thanked my team for praying for us and said, "All I know is this: The rope holds." When it was my turn to be crushed in the crucible of suffering, all the books in my library about the problem of pain and the theology of evil meant nothing. All I knew was that the rope of faith was holding me up. I was sharing the fellowship of suffering with my Lord. I have never felt closer to him before or since.

> **All I knew was that the rope of faith was holding me up.**

Our season of Solemn Assembly was a much more difficult season of suffering. God seemed to have abandoned his post. Confusion reigned. I could not hear God's voice. At no time during this season did I experience the warm, comforting presence of a gentle Shepherd. Satan's presence and power seemed much more real to me during those troubled days in our church. I battled fear and discouragement. Tears flowed for almost no reason at all. I began to stoop, finding it difficult to stand up straight. Every time I thought we had climbed the last hill, another hill had to be taken. It was not that the rope was not holding. I could not find the rope at all.

As terrible as our bout with cancer was, a sweetness came within the struggle. I felt the Shepherd carry me. The difficult year in our church had no sweetness to it, no warm feelings of spiritual closeness. Just pain.

Yet today, as I look back on that difficult season, I clearly see God's hidden hand. I see now that we were in an intense spiritual battle, where the future of our church hung in the balance. It seemed God and Satan had struck a deal similar to the one they shook on regarding Job. Satan seemed to have permission to assault us, even while the normal comforts of God's presence appeared to be withdrawn. I see now that God was asking us: "Will you trust me? Will you believe in me even when you cannot see and feel me? Will you believe in my power to deliver when Satan's power to destroy seems so much more real?"

During these times of naked faith, when what we see and feel finds no coherence with what we say we believe, we come to know our God most intimately. Thankfully, we said yes to those hard questions God had for us, and kept walking, trusting, and hoping against hope that God would spare our church from a messy relational split.

I read the prophet Habakkuk more than once during those long days. Habakkuk closes his prophecy with a prayer, where he confesses his abject terror as he realizes that the judgement of God is upon him. Nothing his eyes could see stirred faith. Everything told him that God had left Israel forever. Yet Habakkuk chooses to trust anyway, expressing his faith with these timeless words:

> Though the fig tree does not bud and there are no grapes on the vines, though the olive crop fails and the fields produce no food, though there are no sheep in the pen and no cattle in the stalls, yet I will rejoice in the LORD, I will be joyful in God my Savior.[9]

WHEN YOU CAN'T SEE THE ROPE

The Danish theologian Søren Kierkegaard once compared faith to a blind leap in the dark. I have never liked that definition because the Christian faith is rooted in the historical reality of Christ's life, death, and resurrection. Yet sometimes it does feel as if we must leap into the abyss of nothingness and lunge for a rope we cannot see. These times of naked faith are light years away experientially from the tender times when the good Shepherd carries us through the valley of our fears. These dark nights of the soul are just as important in our quest to know Jesus. They teach us that he is always present, even when we cannot feel him or see him or hear him.

Several Sundays ago we were enjoying an exceptional worship service. God's presence, to borrow a phrase from the Puritans, was thick among us. The passion to preach had returned to me again. We had had a full, satisfying week working well together as a staff team. And many new ministries were beginning to launch. My eyes became moist as I reflected on where we had been just a year before. God had delivered us.

The sweetness of his presence among us was all the more enjoyable after suffering through the absence of his presence the year before.

Job, in the final words of the epic book that tells of his own journey through suffering, admits, "My ears had heard of you but now my eyes have seen you."[10] Job had moved beyond disappointment into intimacy with his God. He never got any good answers to his many legitimate questions. All he received was a deeper fellowship with his Creator. And that was good enough for him.

I have watched hundreds of Christian men and women walk through the valley of the shadow of death and pain. Most of them emerge from the shadows with a significantly more intimate relationship with Jesus. But not everyone does. Some never leave the shadows at all. If a common denominator can be found in those who encounter Christ in suffering, it is a willingness to choose to trust when all of life screams that they should not. The essential character trait I find in those who suffer redemptively is a humble willingness to leave some questions unanswered, and a quiet decision to believe that God is good even when the evidence says otherwise. Those who allow their disappointment with God to deepen their love of God will understand what Martin Luther meant when he wrote, "Do not begrudge affliction. It is for your good. Affliction teaches you to experience and understand how faithful, true and mighty are the comforting words of God." The reformer went on to say, "I myself owe my adversary many thanks for beating and frightening me because these pains have turned me to God . . . driving me to a goal I should never have reached."

Embracing the Paradox of Pain

One of the paradoxes of pain is that God does not cause evil, but he does sovereignly use evil to draw us closer to himself. The biblical characters did not seem to have nearly as much trouble embracing this paradox as we do.

Joseph understood this mystery. "You intended to harm me," he tells the brothers who had sold him into slavery, "but God intended it for good to accomplish what is now being done."[11] Peter does not flinch when he tells the Jews that Jesus "was handed over to you by God's set purpose and foreknowledge; and you, with the help of wicked men, put him to death by nailing him to the cross."[12] The nails evil men drove into the hands and feet of Christ were the very tools God used to rid the world of sin. This must have been what Paul was thinking when he wrote, "We know that in all things God works for the good of those who love him."[13]

Disappointment with God becomes deeper intimacy with God only when we choose to live within this mystery. Did God cause the evil that has stained my life? No. Can God use this same evil to draw me into the fellowship of his sufferings? Yes.

These are the lessons of the Bible. But do they work this way in real life? I decided to find out by asking this question to two families I know who have suffered more than most.

BOB AND EILEEN

Bob is a professor at the University of Tennessee School of Veterinary Medicine. A gifted, friendly man with a love for people as well as animals, Bob was a self-described nominal church-goer who dutifully put in his hour per week of religion for twenty years but never got much out of it. Then his wife Eileen was diagnosed with breast cancer. They joined me in my office on a windy Friday afternoon a year after the diagnosis to talk about how cancer has touched their lives and their faith. Eileen, a mother of two teenagers with a pretty good backhand and a passion for discipling children, was in the middle of her final rounds of chemotherapy when we spoke.

I was a bit nervous as we sat down together. Our last conversation had been a brief one—Eileen had said she had made the mistake of finding a report on her cancer on the Internet that did not give her very good odds of surviving. How was she coping? Was she depressed? Angry? Or had she found peace? Eileen looked thinner and more tired than I remembered her being, yet her blue eyes radiated inner peace. A tasteful brunette wig covered up the hair loss that every cancer patient knows too well. She and Bob both smiled as they sat down on the couch in my office; and as they smiled I felt the awkwardness drain away.

"Once I got over the original shock," she began, "the Lord moved in. It was an odd sensation. I felt a real closeness to the Lord. There was sadness . . . perhaps I wouldn't see my children grow up. But I have not felt fear."

Bob reached for Eileen's hand as she continued. "I was humbled and touched that the Lord was going to use my cancer in such a mighty way."

I had not expected this response. Bob, seeing the perplexed look on his pastor's face, broke in. "I'll never forget sitting on the bed next to her thinking, 'My wife may die from this.' She said, 'Robert, so many things are going to happen from this, just you wait.'" He paused, squeezed Eileen's hand, and allowed a wave of emotion to wash over him.

"God was in that room," he continued. "I felt it. It was a turning point for me spiritually." Bob now believes that he never had a genuine relationship with Jesus through all those years of church going. God used the cancer to draw him beyond religion into an intimate relationship with himself.

"I once asked God, 'Why did you let Eileen get cancer?'" Bob remembers. "I'll never forget the answer. God said, 'Because you needed saving.'" Bob has been a Christian now for over a year. I had the joy of baptizing him on a recent Sunday. Suffering has continued to deepen Bob's fellowship with his suffering Savior. He handed me a piece of paper with the word *Suffering* written on the top. Beneath it he listed all the ways God had used his wife's cancer in his life.

Suffering. . .

> *Has made me a member of a "fraternity" with which I have had no previous experience.*
>
> *Has taught me how to talk to and understand other members of the "fraternity of sufferers."*
>
> *Has lessened my focus on the distant future, and heightened my focus on this month and this year.*
>
> *Has united my wife and me against a common enemy, and made it easier for us to talk about everything.*
>
> *Has united my wife and me in our desire and quest to better know a common friend (Jesus).*
>
> *Has made me less cynical and more understanding of other people and their problems.*
>
> *Has caused me to spend more time praying than ever before.*

Has made my time in prayer more sincere and humble, and has heightened my expectations of at least "hearing the voice on the other end of the line (God)."

Has allowed me to more readily consider things such as miracles that I have previously resisted, and to have faith in things that I cannot see, touch, hear, or even understand.

Has brought me closer to God.

Has brought me to my knees in fear and has made me soar with hope.

Eileen also believes that God is using the cancer in her life to draw her closer to him. "I feel God permitted the cancer, but didn't give it to me. But he is using it for good." She pauses, searching for the right words. "If we didn't have pain and suffering, wouldn't we eventually say, 'I don't need God'?"

Finally, we talked about death.

"I don't think this is going to do me in," Eileen says with a laugh. "But if I do die, I don't think God broke a promise. Either way, it's a win-win situation. If I get better, I win. If I die, I win because I'm with the Lord."

DAVID AND JAMIE

David and Jamie Hahn are on the other side of death. Christy, their fourteen-year-old daughter, lost a two-year fight with leukemia in November of 1995. Christy was a vivacious, life-loving young lady who had a thriving babysitting business—and, incidentally, once talked some younger children into toilet papering my house so she could honestly say she did not do it. (I caught her anyway.) The line for her funeral was so long some people had to stay in the hall during the service.

David and Jamie had walked with us through our ordeal with Bryden, and we now share the strange intimacy that comes from pledging the "fraternity of cancer sufferers." But since David and Jamie had joined a team to plant a sister church in a nearby community, we hadn't connected with them in over a year. "How do you recover from the death of a child?" I wanted to know. "Can there be any greater disappointment with God? Is it possible to find intimate communion with

God even in the valley of suffering like this?" David, a tall, burly man with a deep voice and kind green eyes, eagerly answered my questions.

"I always had a premonition that we were going to lose one of our children," he began softly, his voice trailing off. "It was eerie. Christy fell on the couch one afternoon, dizzy. We thought it was an inner ear infection. It turned out to be leukemia."

"The doctors couldn't figure out what was wrong," Christy's mother remembered. Jamie's bright smile and sparkling blue eyes reminded me of Christy. "I started grieving the day she was diagnosed. We were soul mates. One day in church David and I looked at each other. We knew it was big."

The Hahns fought the cancer for twenty-six months. "When Christy relapsed," Jamie continued, "God told me during a time when the elders were praying for her that he wasn't going to heal her this time. I wasn't angry. God doesn't always heal the way we want."

We sat in silence. These are hard memories to revisit.

"My only suffering is missing her," David said. "She would have been eighteen now, off to college, having boyfriends."

"It's the holding, the aching, the what-ifs and what-could-have-beens that hurt," Jamie admitted.

I asked Jamie and David to explain how they have found God during their suffering. "I only have two choices," Jamie replied. "I can cling to God or I can commit suicide. If I start asking, 'Why, God?' I spiral out of control. So I trust."

"Some days the pain does paralyze me," David added, wiping away a tear. "But suffering is one of God's tools. The impact of Christy's death on my spiritual life was profound. God used Christy's death as a hammer to get my attention. I've become keenly aware of who is in control. Life is more precious than before. My compassion for others has been heightened. I'm a lot more dependent on God than I used to be."

Silence filled the room once more. David swallowed, then continued.

"Suffering makes the joy more acute. Jamie and I see life in a whole new way now. A sunrise, the clouds, these things can make me cry now. I used to just say, 'That's pretty.'"

Jamie smiled again, reminding me once more of the young girl who would have been eighteen. "Even in the hardest times," she said softly, "God is good."

SIGNS, WONDERS, AND CANCER

I have always believed that God meets us in our suffering. Over the past several years I have also come to believe that God wants us to pray for the sick. I have encountered God as a healing God and seen him intervene in pretty dramatic ways.[14] When you begin to experience God's yeses in answer to prayers for healing, it can be even harder to accept his nos. When we know and believe that God can and does heal it is confusing when he chooses not to heal. Christians from spiritual traditions that place a strong emphasis on healing ministry sometimes suffer the most when God does not heal, especially when they have been taught that their faith is somehow linked with the success or failure of their prayers.

John Wimber, the founder of the Vineyard movement, wrote several best-selling books on healing in the 1980s. The healing ministry has found its way back into so many evangelical churches in part because of this man. Through tapes, books, and conferences Wimber spread his message of "power evangelism," the belief that the preaching of the Gospel should be accompanied by the signs and wonders of healing and deliverance.

During the final five years of his life, Wimber suffered through a heart attack, a stroke, and cancer. Two years after being diagnosed with an inoperable tumor, he wrote an article called "Signs, Wonders, and Cancer." He ended the piece with these words:

> While I was being treated for cancer, someone wrote me a letter asking, "Do you still believe in healing now that you've got cancer?" I wrote back: "Yes! I do." And the truth is, I do.
>
> I also believe in pain. Both are found in the Word of God. In the year I spent battling cancer God purged me of a lot of habits and attitudes that weren't right, and through it I grew stronger as a Christian. Some of my greatest spiritual advances in spiritual maturity came as I embraced the pain—as each day I had to

choose to allow God to accomplish his work in me by any method, even adversity. . . .

Being through the valley of the shadow is frightening. Its uncertainties keep you alert to every changing scenario. I began to cling to every nuance of the doctor's words, shrugs, and grimaces; I experienced the full range of emotions that go with life-threatening illness. I wept as I saw my utter need to depend on God. . . . I had to embrace the truth that I could not control my life. . . . I also found that the view from the valley gave me a focus on Christ that I would not have found any other way.[15]

CHOOSING TO SUFFER REDEMPTIVELY

After surveying the stories we have considered in this chapter, I cannot help but notice the important role of individual choice in redemptive suffering. Wimber *chose* to embrace the truth that he could not control his life. Jamie and David *chose* to cling to God. Bob and Eileen *chose* to believe that God was going to use their suffering for good. Habakkuk *chose* to trust in God even when the crops failed and invaders stormed upon his city.

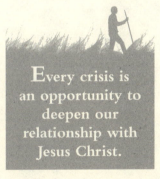

Every crisis is an opportunity to deepen our relationship with Jesus Christ.

We inhabit a fallen planet. Murphy was at least partly right—whatever can go wrong, probably will at some point. We cannot inoculate ourselves from pain. No one asks us whether or not we want to hurt. We do not get to vote on the matter. Suffering simply happens. We can do nothing about it. Ironically, some of the worst suffering in life comes to people who are preoccupied with protecting themselves from suffering! We cannot choose when and how we will suffer. We can, however, choose how we will respond to it.

LESSONS FROM AMY'S DOGWOOD

The Chinese word for "crisis" means "opportunity." Every crisis is an opportunity to deepen our relationship with Jesus Christ. Every crisis also provides an opportunity to walk away from him. I am reminded of this every time I look out my office window at Amy's dogwood. Mark and his family planted the tree to honor the memory of their precious daughter. Each April, the dormant branches of Amy's dogwood awaken from their winter death and adorn themselves with the life-giving pastels of an east Tennessee spring. Life comes from death. This simple truth is woven into the tapestry of our seasons. It is woven into the tapestry of our souls, as well. Do we believe it?

NINE

RESCUED

The movie *Saving Private Ryan* begins where it ends—in a windswept French graveyard lined with hundreds of white tombstones, nestled in the quiet farmland just beyond the beaches of Normandy. An old man, obviously a veteran of World War II, walks with tortured steps amidst the graves until he finds the marker of the man he has come to honor. Two and a half hours later, we find out why.

The old man is James Ryan, who served as an army private in the Normandy invasion fifty years earlier. The tombstone Ryan is seeking bears the name of Captain John Miller, the school-teacher-turned-soldier who led the mission through occupied France to find Private Ryan and send him home. Captain Miller and the men he led on the rescue mission all died. Ryan survived and returns to Normandy fifty years later to remember the men who gave their life for him. The film ends by returning to the Normandy cemetery where James Ryan is overcome with emotion as he walks away from his rescuer's grave.

RESCUED

The emotions Private Ryan must have felt as he wept beside John Miller's grave are similar to the ones we feel when we recognize how Jesus spares our lives from sin, pain, and even death. Jesus Christ came to rescue us. The basic meaning of the word "salvation" in the Bible is "to experience rescue."[1] But what are we rescued from when Christ saves us?

We are saved from the penalty of sin, certainly. But the biblical idea of salvation is much broader than that. Biblical salvation has the idea of being rescued from an enemy who wants to destroy every part of us— body, mind, and soul.

LIVING BETWEEN THE TIMES

I waited nearly a year before I saw *Saving Private Ryan*. I had heard that the film was incredibly violent, and I wasn't sure I wanted to expose my mind to that much bloodshed. Yet the more I heard about the movie, the more I felt compelled to watch it.

Saving Private Ryan takes place after D-Day and before VE-Day. Military experts knew that Hitler had lost the war when the Allied troops took Normandy Beach and established a beachhead in occupied France. Nevertheless, a long, bloody year of battle lay ahead before the war finally came to an end. That historic day is called VE-Day.

Theologian Oscar Cullman compared the time in World War II between D-Day and VE-Day to the time we now live between the first and second comings of Christ.[2] Jesus "invaded" a rebellious planet when he came to earth as the Son of Man. His death on the cross assured ultimate victory over Satan, the tyrant whose kingdom extends over all the earth. He left behind an invading army—the church— with the mission of taking back every occupied tribe and nation on the earth.

The war is not yet over. Satan, fueled by the maniacal rage of a defeated despot, is practicing his own hellish scorched earth policy, murdering and maiming anyone he can, even as he beats his retreat and prepares for his final doom at the second coming of Christ.

Sometimes I'm discouraged when Satan, a defeated foe, is still able to do so much damage. I chose to watch *Saving Private Ryan* to remind me of how intense war between the times can be. I wasn't disappointed. We can't appreciate what it means to be saved until we understand that we, like Private James Ryan, are fighting a wicked enemy in a world ruled by dark powers.

A Planet in Revolt

But wait a minute! Isn't Jesus the Lord of the universe? Yes he is. But the universe is in revolt, held captive by the powers of Satan. Jesus himself calls Satan "the prince of this world."[3] John teaches that the entire world is "under the control of the evil one"[4] while Paul calls Satan "the god of this age."[5] Jesus came, however, "to destroy the devil's work" and "proclaim freedom for the prisoners."[6] He came to rescue us from our enemy.

What happens when I am saved? Yes, my sins are forgiven. Thank God for that! But salvation is much more than a change in my legal status before God. *Salvation is being rescued!* Private Ryan would have been murdered or taken captive by his enemy had Captain Miller not saved him. He was saved from death or torture. And so are we when Christ saves us. "The word 'saved' meant simply to be saved ... from the scourges and afflictions of Satan."[7]

Does God Kill Little Girls?

A strange teaching has crept into the church that attributes "the scourges and afflictions of Satan" to the good purposes of God. Three teenage girls and one of their fathers died on an end of the summer trip to a theme park. A semi-truck slammed into the back of their church van and crushed them. At their funeral, someone said to me, "God must have wanted them in heaven, so he took them."

I do not think so. The comforting teaching we considered in the last chapter—that God is so sovereign he can use evil for good—*does not* teach that God causes evil to occur. God does not crush little girls on the way to church retreats. Satan does. God then works through the tragedy to bring healing.

Sickness and suffering are used by God, but they are not sent by God. Sickness is one of the ways Satan punishes the people he hates. Disease is one of the ways he rules his wicked realm. When Jesus healed a crippled woman, he called her a daughter of Abraham "whom Satan has kept bound for eighteen long years."[8] Peter describes how

> Sickness and suffering are used by God, but they are not sent by God.

Jesus "went around doing good and healing all who were under the power of the devil."[9] Healing is one of the ways Jesus rescues us from the devil's power. He heals us because he loves us and does not like to see us suffer.

TO GOD BE THE GLORY

On Easter Sunday, April 11, 1993 this headline and subheading appeared on the front page of the *Chattanooga News-Free Press:*

> Michele Rasnake Conquers Cancer
> Mother, 31, reports more than 20 tumors cured

The article describes how God rescued her from her disease.

> Last October, doctors found 20 cancerous tumors in Michele Rasnake's body, located in her breast, chest, chin, shoulder, arm, spine, pelvis and eight in her liver.
>
> Today she is cancer-free and celebrating Easter with her husband Eddie and four children. The 31-year-old Mrs. Rasnake had given birth to her youngest son only a few weeks before she first began experiencing pain last August. Her initial symptoms were back problems, fever and flu-like pains.... On October 2, she was diagnosed with non-Hodgkins T-cell lymphoma, a very rare, aggressive form of cancer.
>
> Mrs. Rasnake remembers having a sense of peace upon hearing the news. "God didn't cause this, but he allowed it to happen," she explained.... Mrs. Rasnake began chemotherapy at Erlanger Medical Center on Oct. 14. Doctors gave her a 40% chance of survival.... As a result of the chemotherapy, Mrs. Rasnake's immune system shut down in November and she was hospitalized for two weeks in protective isolation. Separated from her children, she described the time as the roughest stretch of her illness.
>
> Mrs. Rasnake completed chemotherapy on Dec. 14. On Dec. 17, she and her husband met with doctors at Vanderbilt University Medical Center in Nashville to discuss the possibility of a bone marrow transplant. Doctors gave her a 20% chance of survival because of the unique clinical features of her cancer....

Initially hesitant about the transplant, the Rasnakes decided to go ahead with the treatment in February after Mrs. Rasnake's brother and sister were found to be perfect bone marrow matches for their sister. The young mother was facing a two-month hospital stay followed by a six-month recovery period with the transplant.

Even with the treatment, doctors said Mrs. Rasnake had a 70% chance of relapse within the year. The procedure itself had a 20 to 30% fatality rate. "*I'm going to pull away for one night alone to make tapes and notes for the children to listen to on their significant birthdays and special days like their wedding day. . .and maybe read some of their favorite books to them on tape so they can listen to their mama's voice. As you moms will certainly understand, it will be a miracle if I can do all this without weeping a bucket of tears.*" (February Newsletter).

On March 9, Mrs. Rasnake had the first of three scheduled biopsies done in preparation for the transplant. However, three days later lab reports failed to confirm any malignancy. Doctors did not believe she was in remission, so they scheduled a second biopsy March 18.

Around 3 a.m. that morning, Mrs. Rasnake awoke. She visualized herself being wheeled into the operating room singing the hymn "To God Be the Glory." She sensed God was going to bring her ordeal to an end.

After four hours of surgery that morning, doctors told the Rasnakes they could find no malignant tumors in Mrs. Rasnake's body. On March 23, a Vanderbilt pathologist confirmed she was in remission. . . .

"*The doctors have no good explanation for what has transpired, but we do. We see it as a work of God. We believe she was not in remission and the Lord chose to overrule.*" (March Newsletter).

The Rasnakes credit their recovery to prayer support from friends and God's faithfulness in their lives, in addition to the expertise of the doctors.

The following Sunday I copied the newspaper article and handed it out to our congregation, many of whom had been praying for the

Rasnakes. A palpable sense of awe swept the congregation as the people realized what God had done—he had rescued one of his children from cancer! Seven years later as of this writing, Michele is still cancer-free. "We are so humbled by this tremendous act of grace," Eddie wrote in a follow-up newsletter. "God's goodness is overwhelming."

Like Private Ryan, we experience tender affection for our rescuer when Jesus delivers us from our diseases. "Praise the LORD, O my soul . . . who forgives all your sins and heals all your diseases,"[10] cried King David, perhaps after he had encountered the mercies of Jehovah-Rapha, the God Who Heals. It feels good to be rescued. Healing us is one of the ways Jesus lets us know how much he cares for us.

THE COMPASSIONATE HEALER

When word came to Jesus that his beloved cousin John had been brutally martyred by thugs working the dungeon under Herod Antipas's sprawling estate, he "withdrew by boat privately to a solitary place."[11] What a lonely, desolate row across the gray waters of the Sea of Galilee that must have been. John's murder foreshadowed his own. Time was running out. He desperately needed to be alone with his Abba. To weep, perhaps? To cry out in anger at the injustice of it all? We will never know.

What we do know is that he never made it to that lonely place. "When Jesus landed and saw a large crowd, he had compassion on them and healed their sick."[12] The New Testament word for compassion literally means "from the gut." The Greek word is used to describe a gasp from a man overwhelmed by sorrow, or the groan of a woman in labor. Jesus healed because suffering people broke his heart. His healing ministry flowed out of his deep sorrow for the pain of his suffering people, crippled and maimed by the god of this world. The apostle Matthew, writing his reflections on the life and ministry of his Master, would single out compassion as the dominant motive for all he said and did.

> Jesus went through all the towns and villages, teaching in their synagogues, preaching the good news of the kingdom and healing every disease and sickness. When he saw the crowds, he had compassion on them, because they where harassed and helpless, like sheep without a shepherd.[13]

REBUKING SICKNESS?

One Sunday morning as I prepared to preach, I felt flu-like symptoms spreading across my body. My head began to ache, my stomach was upset, and I could tell I was beginning to have a fever. I used to simply resign myself to sickness. On a day like this, I would have expected to feel lousy for several days, struggled through the morning, and then gone home to bed.

Not anymore. I now believe that sickness is an affliction from Satan. I am learning to be more aggressive in resisting sickness in my own life and in the life of the people I shepherd. When Peter's mother-in-law spiked a life-threatening fever, Jesus "bent over her and rebuked the fever, and it left her."[14] Jesus did not passively receive sickness. He aggressively confronted it. And that is what I am learning to do. During the second service that Sunday I prayed, "Jesus, you died to save me from all the effects of sin. I'm not just going to sit here and wait until I get sick. By the power and authority of your mighty name I rebuke this sickness and ask that you protect your servant from any strategy of the evil one against me. In your mighty name I pray, Amen." By the time I finished the sermon I was feeling fine again. Driving home from church that day I thanked Jesus for his compassion toward me. He had rescued me from sickness. And I felt close to him.

> Jesus did not passively receive sickness. He aggressively confronted it.

Am I healed every time I pray? No. Remember: We are living in between the times. The power of the kingdom is here only in part. We still have a worthy foe. Christ has not yet returned to banish evil altogether. Full rescue from the effects of sin will not occur in this life. But when he does heal me, I feel his compassion. And my love for him swells in return.

Sometimes we encounter the compassion of Christ as we walk *through* a trial. Other times we meet his compassion when he rescues us *from* a trial. As a professional observer of people's spiritual journeys, I have noticed that God often touches us with healing when we are at the end of our rope and just need some tangible evidence that he really does care.

PLEASE HEAL MY CHILD

Beth's son Reed was diagnosed with fluid on the brain four months into her first pregnancy. "All the ventricles in the brain were filled with fluid, pointing to the hydrocephalic birth defect that so many fear," she recalled. "My life was one big mess during this time due to some very immature and sinful decisions."

Her doctor suggested she abort Reed, but Beth refused. Depressed over the prospect of her little boy's dismal future, she had it out with God one November afternoon while mulching leaves. "I asked God to heal my child, and if that was not possible, I thanked him for choosing me to be his mom."

Four weeks before Reed was born, God healed him. "The radiologist asked the nurse to call for my doctor," Beth remembers. "When he arrived, he looked in the monitor. *The fluid was gone in all the ventricles!*" Her doctor told her he had no explanation for what had happened. "I laid there with tears flowing and the only thing that could come from my mouth was, 'It's God.' How awesome he is to heal my child." Beth met the gentle Healer of Nazareth in a time in her life when she really needed to know God still loved her despite her mistakes. Jesus saw Beth suffer. And he rescued her.

JAN

"Jan has MS."

It was May of 1996. Jan, a brand-new believer with a ravenous hunger for Scripture and a throbbing heart for her lost coworkers, had just received the worst news anyone could ever hear.

"This is what I heard in the diagnosis," Jan told me on a steamy August afternoon, three years into her battle with one of life's most debilitating diseases. "First, there is no cure. Second, you will have MS all your life. Third, there is the possibility you will get worse. And fourth, you will never get back all your functioning."

Jan had little hope for healing at first. "I decided I was going to be the best sufferer there's ever been," she grinned. Two years passed. She became fatigued, and started to lose her ability to walk.

Then Jan noticed that her disease had a "personality." "I started to see patterns that were very suspicious," she recalls. "I noticed that the attacks would happen around ministry times." During this time Jan was asked to stand and give a testimony at our church's ten-year anniversary celebration. "I had great trouble walking that day, and I really didn't think I could stand through my testimony." She laughed as she admitted that she had picked up the phone to call me and tell me she could not speak at the celebration. God stopped her though, and she prayed for strength instead. When it came her turn to speak, "my legs turned to steel pillars! I could have stood for hours."

Jan began to realize that she really had not asked God to rescue her from this disease. Then a strange thing happened. Jan, a very gifted Bible teacher, was speaking at a women's retreat. Every woman present was suffering from a physical illness. "As I listened during our discussion times I was very disturbed with what I heard. I heard myself. These dear women were pleading for the right to suffer with their disease. . . . Some of the women even spoke with an eerie tenderness toward their affliction, almost like wearing it as a badge of honor. This was very unsettling."

Jan realized that she had assumed that MS was God's will for her life. In fact, she had let MS become a part of her identity. Jan began to ask Jesus to rescue her from the affliction called Multiple Sclerosis. God led her into a season of deep communion with him that fanned the flames of her spiritual passion. She laid down many of her ministry activities and began spending long hours in prayer and in the Word. "I began to experience a new kind of freedom and joy in him. The closer he let me get, the more of him I wanted. I started to feel an almost unbelievable desire for him."

Then, a surprise. "I was getting healthier!" she beamed. "What I am finding is that as I grow in the Word I am getting better, both physically and spiritually." Jan still does have periodic bouts with the disease. But they do not debilitate her as they once did. She confided in me that she is gaining so much strength that she might lose her disability pension!

I asked Jan how her journey in healing has influenced her walk with Christ. "My story is not really about my health," she responds thoughtfully. "It's about Christ owning me. My health is a side benefit."

Jan later wrote me these words, to put our discussion into perspective. "It is just like what Shadrach, Meshach, and Abedego said: 'If it be so, the God whom I serve is able to deliver me from MS, and he will deliver me out of its hand, O king of this world. But even if he does not, let it be known, that I am not going to serve your gods or worship the image that you have set before me.' Christ is the author of my faith. It is in him I believe."

HEALING DAMAGED EMOTIONS

Some of the most powerfully intimate encounters with Christ as Healer occur when we pray for emotional healing. All pain is caused by our enemy. Jesus is as interested in healing damaged emotions as he is in healing damaged bodies. Counselor David Seamands compares our inner worlds to the rings in a giant redwood tree. Naturalists know that each ring represents a year in the developmental history of the tree. They can tell which years suffered drought, which had too much rain, which year saw the tree struck by lightning.

"All of this lies embedded in the heart of the tree, representing an autobiography of its growth. And that is the way with us. Just a few minutes beneath the protective bark, the concealing, protective mask, are the recorded rings of our lives," Seamands reminds us. "There are the scars of ancient, painful hurts . . . the pressure of a painful, repressed memory. . . . In the rings of our thoughts and emotions, the record is there; the memories are recorded, and all are alive. . . . They affect the way we look at life and God, at others and ourselves."[15]

Few times are more tender or intimate than when the living Healer gently mends a damaged emotion buried deep within one of his children. Praying for the healing of damaged emotions is one of the most fulfilling parts of my ministry. Sandi and I usually minister this way together. We find that healing prayer for damaged emotions is most effective when the person seeking prayer is already on the journey with close brothers and sisters. When the normal means of grace (prayer, fellowship, fasting, the study of Scripture, worship, serving, the sacraments) have taken the wounded person as far as they can, intervention is needed. One of the life rings needs to be healed before the journey can resume again.

The Kiss of Intimacy

Tammy sought prayer after hitting a spiritual plateau. We asked the Holy Spirit to reveal to us the damaged emotions that were crippling Tammy's spiritual growth. We asked the Holy Spirit to uncover Tammy's inner wounds.

A flood of memories began to fill Tammy's mind. Gradually, the images slowed, until she found herself reflecting on a painful scene by her father's sickbed. "No," she cried out. "I don't want to go there." Slowly, painfully, the wound was exposed. Tammy's father had died a long, slow death, slipping into a coma that he never recovered from. As Tammy stayed in the memory, waves of anger rolled over her. Tammy felt orphaned, abandoned by the dying man who was her father. Because she knew her father could not help his sickness, she had never allowed herself to feel rage at him. But the little girl that clung to his bedside that day, begging him to wake up, did not know better. A deep internal anger had been eating away at Tammy ever since. Finally, the waves of emotion subsided. Tammy found herself, in her mind's eye, empty and alone but no longer angry, standing beside her father's still body.

We asked Jesus to visit this exposed emotional wound and heal it. Tammy sat quietly for many moments. "What's happening?" I asked. Tammy wiped tears from her eyes.

"Jesus is holding me. He is telling me that he will take care of me. He is telling me he wants to be intimate with me. And . . . we are dancing. He is holding me in his arms, and we are dancing around the room."

Tammy's journey, like yours and mine, is not yet finished. But she is on the journey again, refreshed by the healing touch of a dancing Savior.

Pledging the Fraternity of Men

My own journey through emotional healing was more of a process than an event. Buried deep within my driven exterior was a fear of failing in the world of men. One of the reasons I was obsessed with succeeding was because I saw success as the entrance fee one had to pay to join the fraternity of real men. The dark side of this bent longing was my inability to relate well to other men. At some level I saw other men as competitors. I was especially threatened by strong, confident men for fear that they might take my much-desired place in the elusive inner ring of true men. Or perhaps I feared they would really get to know me and expose me as a fraud, a would-be man riddled with insecurity.

Beneath these fears lurked a perplexing internal riddle: Just what is a true man anyway? The men I had admired the most were military heroes, sports stars, and corporate tycoons. I had no models of manhood that seemed to fit who I was finding myself to be: creative, reflective, a bit mystical, prone to think a bit too much about the complexities of life, while at the same time possessing an enormous vision for the progress of the kingdom of God.

These fears began to seep up through the cracks of my psyche as my counselor and I spent time together. I never became aware of a specific time God performed surgery on one of my fractured life rings. I never had an experience like Tammy's. Yet after a year of prayer, Scripture reading, and sharing my heart, I began to notice that my fear of men was subsiding. In its place I found a growing love and compassion for my brothers in the fraternity of men. My grasp of what a true man could be was broadening, and I became more at peace with the unique person God made me to be.

About the same time, God began to give me relationships with a number of men in our city who were spiritually awakening and eager to learn more about the way of Christ. Today, my relationships with these men are some of the most enjoyable parts of my ministry. Ironically, most of these men are strong, successful leaders—the very type of men I most feared a few years ago. I now find great pleasure in encouraging them beyond their spiritual comfort zones and speaking the hard things they need to hear to follow after Christ. God is healing me.

THE COURAGE TO EMBRACE THE PARADOX

When Captain John Miller and his weary men finally found Private James Ryan and announced their intention to rescue him, they met an unexpected response. He did not want to be rescued. Sometimes we approach healing the same way. We act as if we really do not want to be healed. Wary of getting our hopes dashed by asking and not receiving, we do not ask at all.

Dare we face the paradox? We have no other choice if we are to honestly engage Scriptures that teach us to think in terms of both-and and not either-or. God commands that we pray for healing. He warns us that the answer will often be no.

Disappointment with God is inevitable on this planet in revolt. We cannot hide from pain and suffering. We must learn to suffer redemptively by choosing to believe in God's goodness when the facts scream otherwise. And we must have the faith to risk being rescued. Deep within this paradox lies the secret to journeying long with God.

God commands that we pray for healing. He warns us that the answer will often be no.

TEN

FINISHING THE QUEST

hree of the nation's premier preachers spoke at the midweek chapel services during my middle year of seminary. Within the next few years, each of them had committed adultery and brought disgrace to their families and their ministries. Why do people become unfaithful to the person they love?

The hymn writer was dead-on when he said that our hearts are prone to wander.[1] Faced with the hard, painful work required to create true intimacy in marriage, many step off the road less traveled and settle for the intoxicating pleasures of new romance instead. Television shows and movies, obsessed with glorifying "affairs," rarely tell us the rest of the story. They do not bother to fast-forward the tape and let us see what miserably selfish marriages unfaithful people create with each other.

After witnessing too many marriages collapse under the weight of unfaithfulness, I have changed the way I conduct a wedding ceremony. Now I pause before reciting the wedding vows and say, "You realize that all the powers of hell will be unleashed against you to incite you to break these vows. Think about what you are saying. It is a holy thing to pledge your lifelong commitment to one another before God and others. Do not take this moment lightly."

Many couples who do manage to remain married for the entire journey end up more like roommates than lovers. Think about it: How many married couples do you know who are still growing in oneness twenty or thirty years after the wedding day?

The second law of thermodynamics applies to relationships as well as to energy: Both have a natural tendency to fall apart. How do we prevent relational entropy?

Sandi and I have tried to cultivate a lifestyle that keeps our marriage growing and our hearts committed to one another on the pilgrimage to intimacy. We have disciplined ourselves to make small choices that, over time, keep our marriage growing and guard our hearts from the seductive attraction of lesser lovers. We spend time together; we go on a date once a week; we pray together; and we talk on the phone when one of us is traveling.

We guard our hearts for one another also through several other disciplines: I never counsel women alone with the door closed, for example, nor will I drive in a car with only a woman. I do not watch or read sexually explicit material, and I have several brothers who hold me accountable to purity. Sandi has specific disciplines that help her guard her heart, too.

Discipline alone is not enough. We must also have seasons of romance and passion—to forget the rest of the world so all that matters is the two of us. These special rendezvous are essential ingredients in building faithfulness in our marriage. We try to schedule getaways several times a year.

Spiritual adultery is no less common than physical adultery. How easily our hearts run to the lesser gods of our addictions! How hard it is to stay faithful to the One we have pledged our life to. Some people are so seduced by a lesser lover that they abandon their relationship with Christ altogether. Many more settle into a heartless religiosity, devoid of power and spirit. How do we stay faithful to the One we love? Again we are wise to listen to the wisdom of both our evangelical and our charismatic brothers and sisters.

Evangelicals call us to a disciplined lifestyle of daily choices—choices to spend time with the Lord, to guard our hearts from the things that steal our intimacy and lure us away from true faith.

Charismatics remind us that disciplined commitment must be wedded with intimate encounters with our Beloved, special touches of his presence that awaken our longing for him and rekindle dormant spiritual desires.

THE QUEST

The spiritual life, like marriage, is a pilgrimage into intimacy. This is why we often use words like *journey, walk, pilgrimage,* and *warfare* to describe our experience with Jesus. We know in our hearts what the Bible affirms on its pages: The spiritual journey is a difficult one. Great dangers await those who dare commit themselves to a lifelong pursuit of the Savior. Yet, in the end we also know the quest is well worth the sacrifice.

The Quest for the Holy Grail, a pilgrimage epic recounting the stories of the legendary King Arthur, has been told and retold by Christians for eight hundred years. On one level it is the story of King Arthur's knights searching for the cup of the Last Supper. But at a deeper level the ancient legend is an allegory of Christian pilgrimage.

The Holy Grail is the cup Jesus drank from at the Last Supper. Legend has it that Joseph of Arimathea brought the cup to Great Britain, where it lay hidden for centuries. One evening, as the Knights of the Round Table gather in King Arthur's Court to celebrate the Feast of Pentecost, the Holy Grail appears to them in a vision. The knights set out on a quest to find the Grail and bring it back. Their journey is fraught with peril. The brave warriors encounter marauding armies, seductress damsels, demonic spirits, a pair of lions, a blind king, and a Black Knight.

Sir Lancelot, weighed down with the guilt of his adultery with King Arthur's wife, Queen Guinevere, fails in the quest and returns home. Other knights fall in defeat as well. Finally Sir Galahad retrieves the Grail from its castle. When he does, the Fisher King, who keeps watch over the Grail, is healed from a wound in his thigh, and his lands, ravished with drought, instantly become fertile again. Galahad, his quest fulfilled, peers into the Grail and sees mysteries no human being can imagine. With his heart full of the presence of God, he cries out to be taken to heaven, then dies. Heaven opens, and the Grail disappears.

Many months go by before the story of Galahad's quest reaches the Knights of the Round Table. One version of the legend describes the final scene from the perspective of one of the returning knights.

Half the places at the Round Table were empty, and among those missing were many of the best who used to sit there. And of those who were there, many had wounds and scars, and most were changed in some way from what they had been before. And he thought that the high adventure of the Grail had been a costly one.[2]

The legend offers a fitting parable of our pilgrimage into intimacy with Jesus Christ. Not all who set out on the Quest attain it. Some are felled by the enemies of lust or pride. Others get lost in the dark woods of sin and deceit. Many lack the courage to journey beyond the comfort of their present kingdom. Yet some pilgrims complete the Quest and reach the end of life wounded and scarred, but changed in some way from what they had been before.

THE DANGER OF FAILED PILGRIMAGES

Eugene Peterson, in his book on the spiritual journey aptly titled *A Long Obedience In the Same Direction: Discipleship in an Instant Society*, complains, "The persons whom I lead in worship, among whom I counsel, visit, pray, preach and teach want short cuts. They want me to help them fill out the form that will help them get instant credit (in eternity). . . . The Christian life cannot mature under such conditions."[3]

Spiritual growth has no short cuts. Those who stay faithful to Christ do so because they have made a lifetime of choices to spend time with him and to protect their hearts from lesser gods. Only those who master the disciplines of such a lifestyle are successful on the Quest.

Of course, there are many failed pilgrimages. One of the most touching scenes in the epic story occurs when tragic Sir Lancelot, unable to claim for himself the forgiveness made possible on the cross, abandons his pilgrimage.

"I am a great sinner," said Sir Lancelot, "and the weight of my sin is on my head and on my spirit. I am shut out from God." . . . He knew that for him the Quest was spent and over.[4]

Many who fill churches each Sunday and go through the motions of religion have come to a similar place. For them, the Quest is spent and over. Being religious is not hard. Sustaining a lifelong, intimate friendship with Jesus Christ is. Sprinkled through the pages of the New

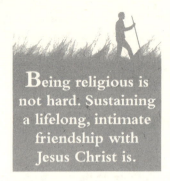

Being religious is not hard. Sustaining a lifelong, intimate friendship with Jesus Christ is.

Testament are hints of journeys never finished. Writing in the final days of his own quest, Paul mournfully acknowledges, "Some . . . have shipwrecked their faith."[5] And the writer of the letter to the Hebrews warns his suffering fellow pilgrims, "See to it, brothers, that none of you has a sinful, unbelieving heart that turns away from the living God."[6]

STAYING IN LOVE

We return to the question with which we began this chapter: How do we stay faithful to the One we love? Before we attempt an answer, let's remind ourselves again that we are talking about a relationship with the living Christ. Many discussions about the spiritual journey devolve too quickly into technique and principles without fully appreciating the *relational* dynamic of spiritual growth. What we are really talking about is staying in love with the most important Person in our lives.

My marriage enjoys many seasons of warm closeness but also many struggles through seasons of wintry distance. Part of this is simply the reality of a very busy life. Yet, when the seasons of closeness are eclipsed more and more frequently by prolonged seasons of distance, I begin to worry about the health of our marriage. Invariably, when we go back and look at the patterns in our life that have resulted in our distancing ourselves from one another, we find that we have not been spending much time together. It is simply not possible to be intimate with another person when you do not spend time together. This is true whether the person is a friend, a child, a spouse, or Jesus Christ.

I enjoy watching people in restaurants, especially when I am traveling and eating alone. You can learn a lot about the health of a marriage by watching how couples interact over a meal. Many couples, especially older ones, no longer seem to enjoy one another's company. One couple I observed recently should have sat at separate tables. The husband buried his head in the sports section while the wife blew smoke rings and stared through a distant window at a half-full parking lot. They ate in silence and left in silence. The restaurant industry seems to have figured out that meal times, which traditionally have been the setting where families bond and reconnect, are no longer designed for that. Now most restaurants have television sets for their customers to watch while they eat. And if you can find a TV-free restaurant, the rock-and-roll background music is often so loud you have to shout across the table.

Yet, look hard enough and you will find a couple savoring their mealtime together. They do not know what to order the first time the waiter comes because they have been so engaged in conversation. These couples are difficult to wait on because every time the waiter returns, he feels he is interrupting something significant. Laughter, intensity, perhaps anger, or even a tear or two shape the conversation. Such couples are rare, but they are the ones who will finish the Quest with an intimate marriage. And that is because they spend intimate time together, not reading the paper or talking about the weather, but penetrating the deep places of their hearts.

Finding the quiet stillness necessary to cultivate a conversational relationship with Christ is far more difficult today than it was even a century ago. The rapid-fire pace of change and an unprecedented explosion in information technology has robbed us of the ability to be still. "Human beings were not built to process what we're going through now," says futurist Watts Wacker.[7] Chew a bit on these mind-blurring facts:

- Today, if you live in New York City, you see 8,000 commercial messages a day.
- The pace of change is so fast on the Internet that cyberspace time must be reckoned in dog years: Just as one year of a dog's life is like seven years of our lives, so one year on the Internet is like seven years in real life.
- Of the Fortune 500 companies on the 1955 list, 70% are out of business today.
- Scientific information doubles every 12 years. General information doubles every two and a half years.
- A weekday edition of the *New York Times* now carries more information than the average seventeenth-century person would have digested in a lifetime.

- About 500 computers were connected to the Internet in 1983. Now there are at least 500 million hosts.
- Approximately 1000 new books are published every day.

Tired yet? "The speed of life is leaving skid marks," quips cultural historian Leonard Sweet.[8] And the joke is not very funny.

I am writing in a secluded mountain cabin on an 1,100-acre farm hidden in the shadows of the Great Smoky Mountains. You cannot get any quieter than this. Nevertheless, since I have been here, I have used a fax machine, email, a cell phone, and that old standby, the telephone. I am thankful for these communication tools. The progress in information technology is certainly one of God's gifts. Yet every blessing has a curse along with it, and the curse of building our house on the information superhighway is the noise that comes from all the traffic.

Life was very difficult in other eras. I would never want to live at any other time than right now. But think how much quieter the world was years ago. Missionary pioneer Hudson Taylor's historic sea voyage to China took six months. Sometimes correspondence on the mission field took a year to complete the loop. When President Lincoln wondered why General McClellan had not attacked the South, he had to get on a horse and go ask him!

Undaunted Courage, the stunning bestseller chronicling the famous Lewis and Clark expedition, reveals a world that moved at a much slower pace and was filled with considerably more time for reflection than our own. We learn that Meriwether Lewis walked much of the journey to the Pacific—his dog, Seaman, beside him—covering as many as thirty miles a day in complete solitude. When the weather cooled, life froze with it, and Lewis and his men settled in until the spring thaw.

> As in many frontier fortifications, life at Fort Clatsop was almost unbearably dull. . . . "Nothing worthy of note today," Lewis wrote in his journal, day after day. With one or two exceptions, his entries recorded the comings and goings and successes or failures of the hunters, the health of the men, the diet, trading sessions with the Clatsops—more often than not unsuccessful— and nothing else.[9]

Our forefathers lived in a much quieter world. None of us would want to return to that world—it was a very scary place without penicillin, chloroform, or CAT scans. But our souls have paid a price for the wonderful technological advances of our century. Today, slowing down, centering in, and being with Jesus is simply harder. And guess what: Life is only going to get noisier.

We who want to complete our Quest need to make intentional choices to spend time with the One we love. We must discipline ourselves to create the safe places where we can share our hearts with Jesus, listen to his words for us, fellowship with him in suffering, laugh with him when he rescues us, and cling to him as we walk through the dark woods that hinder our Quest.

The words of English devotional writer William Law are as irritatingly true today as they were when he wrote them in 1728. "If you will stop here and ask yourself why you are not as devoted as the primitive Christians," Law states bluntly, "your own heart will tell you that it is neither through ignorance nor inability but purely because you never thoroughly intended it."[10] We must intentionally structure our lives so we have time to spend with our beloved One.

RECAPTURING THE STORY

One of the questions I ask couples preparing for marriage is, "What is the redemptive purpose of your marriage?" I explain that God has a special purpose for every marriage, a unique vision that weaves their stories together and prepares them to serve God better than they ever could as singles. I also explain that couples who lose their redemptive vision are in serious trouble. The marriage turns inward and begins to disintegrate rather rapidly.

Vision is the bellows that fans the fires of intimacy in a marriage. When Sandi and I begin to drift apart, usually we have lost sight of the unique Story that God is writing through our home. Our intentional times together reconnect us with our Story. Our eyes begin to look beyond the clutter of the immediate to the horizon of our hopes and dreams. Sandi helps me rediscover my longings as a pastor, father, lover, and writer. I help dust off the desires of her heart that are so often hidden under a pile of laundry. We leave these times renewed, focused, and more deeply in love with one another.

Any relationship, if it is redemptive, exists for purposes beyond the self-pleasure of those who are in it. This is decidedly true in our relationship with Christ. The ultimate goal of spiritual intimacy is not self-fulfillment, but the birth of vision. We draw near to him so that our hearts might become one with his and so that we might better partner with him in fulfilling his own prayer to have done on earth what is done in heaven. Those whose pilgrimages have failed have forgotten this.

When Sir Galahad finally recovered the Grail, the lands of the Fisher King became fruitful once more and the maimed king became whole again. This is the ultimate vision of the Quest: restoring the world and healing its wounded kings. We are all kings in need of healing. And all of our lands are too barren.

Stories like the Quest for the Holy Grail stay alive for centuries because they reflect the deeper story revealed in the Scriptures. This deeper story is the epic tale of people on a journey toward the heart of God. We are all like Abraham, who left his comfortable home to follow God without knowing where he was going or how it would all end. And this, after all, is what lies behind the idea of church. The Greek word for *church* is *ekklesia*—the "called-out ones," people on a pilgrimage.

We must be alone with Jesus so he can retell us the Story. Often, it seems, Abraham forgot his lines. We watch him slip away into a lonely forest to be near the God who called him out. We see Yahweh fill in the details of the story as Abraham passes the tests of each chapter of faith. Later on, the tragic hero David, his spiritual passion matched only by the fire of his lust, slips away to hear the Story again. His great psalms are often nothing more, and nothing less, than the Story retold.

If it is true that our minds are bombarded with eight thousand messages a day, then it makes sense why we so often forget our lines in the drama of redemption. If it is true that the *New York Times* really is crammed full of more facts than Jonathan Edwards saw in his entire seventeenth-century life, it is easy to see why we so often mistake the trivial for the profound.

Now, more than at any other time in history, God's pilgrims must make an intentional effort to sit at the feet of the Storyteller and reconnect with the vision they are partnering with him to fulfill.

One of the most difficult decisions I have made in the ministry was choosing to set aside Thursdays to fast and pray. When I first began taking these days away, everything in me screamed in revolt. "You have too many responsibilities to do this!" the voices in my head yelled. "What kind of a pastor are you who needs to be away from his people?" Now these days away are the anchor of my spiritual life. I come away reminded of the Story and how I fit into it. These times with the One I love encourage me to continue the Quest, no matter what Black Knights await me on Friday.

GUARDING YOUR HEART

Lancelot failed in his quest because he failed to guard his heart. His love for Queen Guinevere, wife of his beloved King Arthur, was greater than his desire to find the Grail. Lancelot meets a priest and confesses his sin to him, but only in part.

> "So then, your sin is confessed," said the priest. "Now swear before God, as you hope for his forgiveness, that you will turn from the Queen's fellowship, and never be with her again, save when others are by."
>
> "I swear," said Sir Lancelot, seeming to tear something raw and bleeding from his breast.
>
> "And that from now on, you will not even wish for her presence, nor be with her in your inmost thoughts," said the priest; and his words fell single and pitiless as axe blows.
>
> "I—swear," said Sir Lancelot. But he prayed within himself, "God help me . . . I have sworn an oath which I cannot keep."[11]

The exercises we practice to protect our hearts from the Guineveres in our lives are called spiritual disciplines. "Train yourself to be godly,"[12] Paul coaches us. We must train to finish the race well. Time spent alone with Jesus, listening to his heart for us and pouring our hearts out to him, is the basic spiritual exercise all other "workouts" must build upon.

We can practice numerous spiritual disciplines and read many good instruction books.

Three disciplines in particular have helped me guard my heart.

THE DISCIPLINE OF CONFESSION

Protestants have often criticized the Roman Catholic doctrine of making confession to a priest on the basis that we do not need to go through another person to be made right with God. While this is true, it overlooks the corresponding truth that confessing sins to one another can help us experience the forgiveness God wants to extend to us. "Confess your sins to each another and pray for each other so that you may be healed,"[13] James instructs.

God does forgive us when we confess our sins privately to him, for "he is faithful and just and will forgive us our sins."[14] Yet there are times when confessing sin to a fellow pilgrim seems to break the power of the sin with greater force. Our adversary hates truth and light. Sometimes our hidden sins, even though we know they have been forgiven, eat away our spiritual tissue like a cancer. Confessing sin to another brings the sin to light and helps the wound heal. Confessed sin brought out in the light of Christian fellowship breaks demonic oppression and protects us from believing lies. When brothers or sisters express forgiveness to us, they embody the forgiveness of Christ.

What we fear the most is often what is the best for us. We are terrified of being exposed, yet that is what our heart longs for. Lancelot failed to make full confession, holding on to his hidden sin even as the priest begged him to confess. Many believers make the same mistake—and, like the knight, fail on their pilgrimage.

THE DISCIPLINE OF ENGAGEMENT

The energy of the soul, left unchecked, drifts rather rapidly towards self-centeredness. I am appalled at how easily I can be concerned only with myself—with *my* feelings, *my* needs, *my* unmet longings, *my* problems and concerns. Self-centeredness is poison to the soul. Because Christ is the essence of other-centeredness, harboring selfishness within our hearts destroys fellowship with him.

Engaging the pain of others reminds me again that the happy ending of the Christian story is not my own fulfillment, but the healing of my fellow knights.

I normally take several trips each year overseas. The stated purpose for these is to assist our missionaries with their important work. Yet these trips have also become a spiritual discipline in my journey. When I visit a country, especially in the Third World, my self-centeredness is exposed for the awful pettiness it really is. How can I fuss about seeing weeds in my lawn or not having extra money for pizza when I have just spent a week with people who make forty dollars a year and live in houses we would not even store our lawnmowers in?

When Fellowship Church began, I spent considerable time each week providing spiritual direction by meeting one-on-one with people. As the church grew and my responsibilities increased, these meetings became fewer and fewer. My time became absorbed with the demanding administrative tasks of leading a large church. During my season of burnout I realized that giving up these times of partnering with my fellow pilgrims as they follow their own quests had robbed me of the gift of engaging in another's story. I have resumed spending several hours a week helping individuals discover and fulfill their spiritual pilgrimage. My heart is the richer for it.

The Discipline of Stories

My love for the Bible initially kept me from valuing the great stories of literature, art, film, and music. I remember once hearing a preacher say approvingly that Robert E. Lee never read anything but the Bible on the grounds that nothing else was worth his time. Why bother with literature when you have the Word of God? I have since discovered that God does speak through lesser stories. He has used songs, poems, books, and movies to sneak behind the curtains of my heart and rearrange some of the props I have hidden there. When I lose the way in the dark wood and forget that the grail is really what I am looking for, the Master Storyteller will use a story to set me on my way again. Good stories are all footnotes to the true Story, as Frederick Buechner has reminded us. In a brilliant chapter on fairy tales Buechner writes,

It is a world of magic and mystery, of deep darkness and flickering starlight. It is a world where terrible things happen and wonderful things too. It is a world where goodness is pitted against evil, love against hate, order against chaos, in a great struggle where often it is hard to be sure who belongs to which side because appearances are endlessly deceptive. Yet for all its confusion and wildness, it is a world where the battle goes ultimately to the good, who live happily ever after, and where in the long run everybody, good and evil alike, becomes known by his true name. . . . That is the fairy tale of the Gospel with, of course, one crucial difference from all other fairy tales, which is the claim made for it that it is true, that it not only happened once upon a time but has kept on happening ever since and is happening still.[15]

Obviously, stories can be dangerous, too. Spending too much time listening to the wrong story can greatly confuse us on our Quest. Yet good stories, and even not-so-good stories carefully read, can help us along the way. Heroes call forth the hero in us. Fools reveal the consequences of poor choices before we make them.

More than once, when the Baggins side of me has wanted to take over, the Tookish side has urged me to press on. When an unforgiving spirit has made me long on justice and short on grace, I often reflect on a magical three hours spent watching the musical version of Victor Hugo's *Les Miserables* and the unfortunate end of Inspector Javert. When the business of ministry grinds the compassion out of my heart, Jan Karon's beloved Father Tim reminds me why I went into the ministry in the first place.[16] And when power and greed try to gain a foothold, Tom Wolfe's Charlie Croker reminds me where that path leads.[17]

Charles Ashworth, whose own journey intersected so powerfully with my own in a dark season of my life, ends his story with words that I took as my own.

I was being tormented now by that old demon, my fear of inadequacy. As I slipped the cross around my neck, I remembered Darrow again. I saw us in the herb-garden, remembered how the word "courage" had echoed in my mind, and suddenly without words I was able to ask for patience, for strength, for the will to endure my difficulties and the wisdom to surmount them.

The demons departed as I stood open before God, and once more I passed through the strait gate to set out along the narrow way in response to my mysterious call. My new life in God's service stretched before me; I knew there could be no turning back. I could only go in the absolute faith that one day His purpose would stand fully revealed, and in the light of that faith the darkness of my anxiety was extinguished. . . . St. Augustine's famous words echoed in my mind: "O God, thou hast made us for thyself, and our hearts are restless until they rest in thee."[18]

ELEVEN

SPECIAL MOMENTS

Jonathan Edwards, the brilliant seventeenth-century theologian whose writings and sermons fanned the flames of the Great Awakening, embodies the commitment to spiritual discipline we considered in the previous chapter. From the time of his conversion Edwards seemed to grasp that Christian growth is "a long obedience in the same direction" requiring earnest devotion. Shortly after his conversion he took time out from his studies at Yale and penned into a notebook seventy spiritual "Resolutions" detailing his plan for spiritual growth. "Resolved," one entry said, "to study the Scriptures so steadily, constantly, and frequently as that I may find and plainly perceive myself to grow in the knowledge of the same." His biographer tells us that he continued to spend thirteen hours a day alone with God, praying, studying, and fasting for most of his adult life.[1] These disciplines sustained him over a difficult life and ministry.

He was dismissed from his duties as pastor of Northhampton's First Church at the age of forty-six and could not find another church that wanted him. His health failing, he took a post as a missionary to the hostile Mohawk Indians along New England's western frontier, then accepted an invitation to become the president of Princeton College, a position much more suited to his gifts. Less than two months after arriving at his happily anticipated new post in the winter of 1758, Edwards was struck down with smallpox. Moments before dying, he called out to Jesus, "my true and never-failing Friend," and comforted his mourning family with a final sentence, "Trust in God and you need not fear."[2]

Jonathan Edwards finished his Quest without turning back.

JONATHAN EDWARDS'S DIVINE ENCOUNTER

We would be mistaken if we attributed Edwards's faithfulness and endurance to his spiritual discipline alone. Scattered along his pilgrimage were moments of intense spiritual pleasure that stirred his "religious affections" for his never-failing Friend. Edwards describes one of those moments in a now-famous paragraph.

> As I rode out into the woods for my health, in 1737, having alighted from my horse in a retired place, as my manner commonly had been, to walk for divine contemplation and prayer, I had a view that was for me extraordinary, of the glory of the Son of God, as Mediator between God and man, and His wonderful, great, full, pure and sweet grace and love.... The Person of Christ appeared ineffably excellent with an excellency great enough to swallow up all thoughts and conceptions, which continued, as near as I can judge, about an hour; such as to keep me a greater part of the time in a flood of tears, and weeping aloud. I felt an ardency of soul to be, what I know not otherwise how to express, emptied and annihilated; to lie in the dust, and to be full of Christ alone.[3]

Edwards did not live on a steady diet of these experiences. But his writings reveal a spiritual journey that included sacred moments of intense spiritual passion. Study the journeys of the heroes of the faith and you will often find that those who finish well have known their share of intimate encounters along the way.

FIRE

Blaise Pascal, the renowned French philosopher and theologian, once encountered the awesome presence of God in such a powerful way that he kept a written record of it sewn in the lining of his jacket. He titled it *The Memorial*.

> In the year of Grace, 1654, on Monday, 23 November ... from about half past ten in the evening until about half past twelve,

FIRE,

God of Abraham, God of Isaac, God of Jacob, not of the philosophers and scholars.

Certitude. Certitude. Feeling. Joy. Peace.

God of Jesus Christ.

Deum meum et Deum vestrum (My God and Your God) . . .

Joy, joy, joy, tears of joy . . .

Let me never be separated from Him.

We keep hold of Him only by the ways taught in the Gospel.

Renunciation, total and sweet.

Total submission to Jesus Christ . . .

Eternally in joy for a day's training on earth.[4]

Christianity is distinct from other religions because of its "theology of presence." We believe in a God who shows up, who breaks into our presence in ways that are always real and sometimes even felt. Sometimes these encounters mark us forever.

"EVERYTHING I HAVE WRITTEN SEEMS LIKE STRAW."

I first encountered the theology of Thomas Aquinas in an Introduction to Philosophy course. Thomas's writings are so brilliant and so exhaustive that we gave the professor lecturing on them a standing ovation when he had finished. (I do not remember whether the applause arose from gratitude or a sense of relief.) Look up this formidable intellectual superman in the library and you will find twenty-five massive volumes of his work.

Christianity is distinct from other religions because of its "theology of presence."

A few months before he died, Aquinas was saying mass when God touched him so powerfully that he could never write another word. This shocked those who knew him, and they begged him to continue writing. "I can't," the great scholar replied. "Everything I have written seems like straw in comparison with what I have seen and what has been revealed to me."[5]

THE "WITH US GOD"

It is Christmas time as I write. Buried beneath layers of noise and hype are ancient carols haunting those who listen with the essence of the season.

O come, O come, Emmanuel. . . .

Emmanuel: God with us. A God who cares enough to draw near. But how near?

I first began to wrestle with this question in 1992 while preaching through the fifth chapter of Romans. The troubling text that began my wrestling match was verse 5: "God has poured out his love into our hearts by the Holy Spirit."

I believed God loves me. But I could not really say I felt that God loves me. And I had never known anything close to a sense of his love being "poured out" into me. I remember closing my Bible, putting on my coat, and heading out for a long walk through the woods. "God," I prayed, "do you want me to experience your love? Should there be times when I really feel you pouring out your love all over me? I'd love that. But it is so far from my experience, I hate to even hope for it."

I sat for a long time on a tree stump and pondered what it really meant to know this Emmanuel, God With Us. How close to us does he really want to get?

SEEKING A DIVINE HUG

I found an answer that made sense in the words of Puritan Thomas Goodwin. He describes a man and his little child walking hand in hand down a country road. The child knows that his father loves him, that he is his father's child, and he is very happy about it. Suddenly the father, moved by some influence the child cannot comprehend, picks him up, cuddles him in his arms, hugs and kisses him, and then puts him down again, and they go walking on together.[6] I realized that this is what I was looking for. I knew the Father loves me, and I lived in the awareness that he is by my side. But I also longed for a divine hug.

As I related in chapter 7, God released my spiritual language in a cabin near the woods that had so often heard my cries to the With Us God. For the first time in my life I literally felt the love of God poured out on and through me. I had always believed theologically that God is near me, for this is the promise of the new covenant. I knew he lives in my heart, and I enjoyed his quiet, internal presence. But that day God hugged me. And I am grateful for it.

I have had a few other divine hugs on my journey. These wonderful experiences, some of which are too personal to relate here, are not the primary means by which I grow spiritually. They occur only rarely, and I can survive without them. But when they come—boy, do they feel good! They remind me that the Quest is worth it and that the One I am questing after is both near and real.

EXTRAORDINARY ASSURANCE

"You received the Spirit of sonship. And by him we cry, '*Abba,* Father.' The Spirit himself testifies with our spirit that we are God's children."[7] I am thankful for the many ways the Spirit quietly assures me of my special place in God's family. God's Spirit tells my spirit that I am Abba's special son when the words from my morning Scripture reading touch the challenges before me in my day. I sense my Abba's affirmation when he answers a private prayer in ways that only he and I know. His Spirit testifies of his love for me in the laughter of my children, the embrace of my wife, the companionship of lifelong friends. These are gifts, and I cherish each of them.

Yet I am learning that sometimes our Abba testifies to his great love for us by overcoming us experientially as well. D. Martyn Lloyd-Jones, the great British preacher who blended passion and doctrine so well, liked to talk about "the customary assurance of the child of God" and "extraordinary assurance."[8] We receive "an unusual sense of the presence of God. . . . What the Holy Spirit does is make real to us the things which we have only believed by faith, the things of which we have had but a kind of indirect certainty only. The Holy Spirit makes these things immediately real."[9]

"I REALIZED THIS WAS THE HAND OF GOD"

Jackie found herself longing for a deeper encounter with the Holy Spirit as she read through the book of Acts. She mentioned this to a friend, who invited her to come to her small group and receive prayer.

"They anointed me with oil and laid hands on me and began to pray," Jackie recalled. "They prayed for God to pour out his Spirit on me, to give me a fresh filling of the Holy Spirit. Almost immediately I became aware of a sensation moving up from my collarbone, up both sides of my throat. It felt like an electronic pulse, but different, softer, alive . . . slow and flowing and deliberate."

God was answering her prayer. "My thoughts of absolute surprise turned to wonder and awe as I realized this was the hand of God. I began to weep. I was overwhelmed by something new in my understanding of God." The Holy Spirit was teaching Jackie experientially what she already knew mentally. "I have always been aware of how high the Lord is. But now I was aware of how near he is. I can't say that any of these thoughts were new to me. God had already revealed them to me in his Word, but it felt like God lifted the veil just a little to let me *see*. I *never* expected him to touch me in a way that I could feel physically. Whew! Since that day I've been more convinced of just how *willing* he is to be known."

Experiences like these are not new among the people of God. Both the Bible and church history repeatedly record special times when the presence of God is manifested in a tangible way. Dr. John Owen, leading Puritan theologian and professor at Oxford, describes these special touches as the Spirit's pouring joy into our hearts. "He secretly infuseth and distils it into the soul," Owen writes, "prevailing against all fears and sorrows, filling it with gladness, exultations, and sometimes with unspeakable raptures of the mind."[10]

> **B**oth the Bible and church history repeatedly record special times when the presence of God is manifested in a tangible way.

TRAVETTA'S STORY

The biblical story reveals a With Us God who chooses to be with his people in some remarkable ways. Even Jesus, who certainly knew the favor of his Father on a moment-by-moment basis, was given the grace of a special touch at his baptism. When he arose from the water, "he saw the Spirit of God descending like a dove and lighting on him. And a voice from heaven said, 'This is my Son, whom I love; with him I am well pleased.'"[11] Even Jesus appreciated special times of tangible affirmation of his Father's love for him.

Travetta is a gifted artist and worship leader whose struggle with arthritis means a daily battle with pain, stiffness, and fatigue. Her physical pain has made it immensely difficult to carry out her calling in worship. She attended a worship conference where the opening speaker preached a message called "Pain, Perplexity, and Promotion" from the book of Job. The talk stirred Travetta deeply.

"After the morning session we broke for lunch," she recalls. "In the exhibit hall I saw a statue of the 'Bride of Christ.' The Bride's heart was thrust toward God with her shoulders back as she yielded herself to him. It was breathtakingly beautiful!"

God was using a work of art to prepare this artist for a special touch of his Spirit. "After lunch we reconvened for a worship time. I felt the Lord ask me if I would accept this season of pain as a refinement for my calling. I raised my hand to say 'yes.' Immediately, my entire body began to tingle with a warm sensation. Then I saw him! Jesus knelt right in front of me with his eyes directly in front of mine, as one would propose marriage. He said he was pleased with my acceptance of this trial and that he was going to be with me literally every step of the way."

Travetta told me that this encounter has encouraged her greatly on a pilgrimage that is steep and often painful.

JUST AS HE DETERMINES

Sometimes Scripture refers to the Holy Spirit's falling upon believers, often with dramatic results. God "took of the Spirit that was on [Moses] and put the Spirit on the seventy elders. When the Spirit rested on them, they prophesied."[12] The Spirit of God fell in a similar way on King Saul, releasing in him the ability to prophesy.[13] When Peter preached to the members of Cornelius's household, "the Holy Spirit came on all who heard the message. . . . They heard them speaking in tongues and praising God."[14] A similar event occurred when Paul ministered the Gospel in Ephesus. Finding a group of disciples who did not know much about the Holy Spirit, Paul prayed for them. "When Paul placed his hands on them, the Holy Spirit came on them, and they spoke in tongues and prophesied."[15]

But does God still touch believers like this? Should we hope for—even pray for—special experiences with the Holy Spirit after conversion?

Determined to find out, I spent two weeks holed up in a seminary library trying to answer this question. I pulled out every book I could find on the Spirit's work in a believer's life and began thumbing through them one-by-one. Most of the students were on vacation, so I spread what eventually became more than a hundred different titles across the library's long oak tables. By the time I was done, I knew the librarians by name and even took a few to lunch to pay "rent" for using their tables. Before long, I had two stacks of books tottering over my laptop and spilling into the study carrel next to me.

The books in the first stack were written by evangelical scholars I had grown up with. Their arguments were comfortable and familiar. Evangelicals look at passages like Acts 10 and Acts 19 and stress the unique, transitional nature of the book of Acts. The Old Covenant is giving way to the New Covenant. The book of Acts records a changing of the guard and we should expect some fireworks to celebrate the initiation of a new kind of kingdom. Once the transition is complete, we should no longer expect spiritual fireworks. I left seminary believing that the Holy Spirit never does today what he did in Ephesus or in Cornelius's house. Yet something did not seem to add up for me as I read through these books again. Even if the book of Acts does record a unique, transitional period in the life of God's people, does that mean the Holy Spirit will never come in a special way on his people again? This conclusion seemed to go beyond the evidence.

The books in the second stack were much less familiar to me. They were written by Pentecostal and charismatic authors. They argued that the pattern we see in Acts—salvation, then a special touch of the Holy Spirit, evidenced by speaking in tongues—is the way the Holy Spirit always works today. This, too, seemed to go too far. Where has the Holy Spirit said that he would do anything the same way twice? The two stacks of books seemed to me to represent two extreme ways to deal with the Holy Spirit's ministry in a believer's life. The first said, "He will *never* work that way again." The second said, "He will *always* work that way again."

I put on my coat, assured the librarian I would clean up before the evening was over, and headed out into a starless winter night. My breath forming little wisps in front of me, I walked around and around the campus, wrestling with my dissatisfaction with both the traditional evangelical and the Pentecostal views on the Spirit's work in a believer's life. On about my third lap around the empty campus, Paul's comment on the sovereignty of the Spirit flashed across my mind. Speaking of the gifts of the Spirit, Paul says, "All these are the work of one and the same Spirit, and he gives them to each one, just as he determines."[16]

"Just as he determines." I think this is the answer to the question, "How does the Holy Spirit work in a believer's life today?" He works just as he determines. He is sovereign—willing and able to do whatever he pleases. We must not say *never* and we must not say *always*. We must say "just as he determines." He will touch you one way and he will touch me another way. We cannot take the "one size fits all" approach to the Spirit's work and ministry. Each encounter is as fresh and new as the need that caused it.

> The Holy Spirit is sovereign—willing and able to do whatever he pleases. We must not say *never* and we must not say *always*.

Why is it that we seem compelled to make the biblical data say more than they really say? Why must we fit the biblical stories into the Procrustean bed of our own theological assumptions? Why must we rush to a formula? The only conclusion we can draw with certainty from the book of Acts is that sometimes the Holy Spirit touches people in a way that causes them to prophesy or speak in tongues. Nothing in the text gives us the right to say *never* or *always*. Let the Spirit be the Spirit. He will touch us *just as he determines*.

The surest way to turn genuine spiritual experience into deadly legalism is to start comparing our divine encounters with God with the experiences of others. No parent treats each child the same way. We should not expect the Spirit to treat any of us exactly the same. When we submit to the sovereignty of the Spirit, a lot of pressure is taken off. I do not have to prove that your experience is wrong because it is not like my own, and you do not have to make sure I have the same experience you have had. When we give each other the grace and freedom to receive the Spirit's gifts and blessings as he determines, the entire body of Christ becomes much healthier. And we are in a better position to receive and appreciate stories like Byron and Betty's.

UNTIL SIX IN THE MORNING

Byron is an elder in our church. He and his wife, Betty, invest the hard-earned hours of their retirement in shepherding the congregation. In the early 1970s, Byron and Betty had been Sunday school teachers in a large, conservative Presbyterian church. During that time, Betty heard a Baptist pastor on the radio teach about healing and so took a friend who suffered from a separated retina to visit this man. As Pastor Frank prayed for healing, a warm breeze blew across the room. The Holy Spirit came upon Betty, and she began to pray in tongues. Pastor Frank said that he would be happy to pray for anyone who wanted to know more about a deeper experience with the Spirit.

The following evening, when she and Byron met with two other couples for their weekly Bible study, one of the husbands began the evening by sharing that he had been reading a book about a deeper experience with the Spirit. Did anybody know what he was talking about? He wanted to know. Betty played a tape the pastor had given her. Deeply stirred, the group called Pastor Frank, who agreed to come and pray for them. He arrived after midnight. Byron, a three-packs-a-day smoker, had been praying for six weeks for a fresh filling of the Spirit and the power to stop smoking. As Pastor Frank began to pray for Byron, Byron collapsed to the floor and began moaning and coughing up phlegm. This went on for two hours. After the coughing subsided, Byron lifted his arms to heaven and began to pray in tongues, not stopping until 6 A.M. Byron believes he was delivered from a demonic stronghold that evening, because he has never smoked since that night.

It has been a quarter of a century now since the Holy Spirit fell upon Byron with such power. Byron and Betty are people of the Word who have walked through many dark forests on their own spiritual pilgrimage. That special evening was a divine gift that strengthened them in their lifelong Quest to know and serve God. They do not talk much about their experiences around our church, content instead to let the Spirit minister to those around them *just as he determines*.

SPECIAL TOUCHES IN COUNSELING

My belief in the sovereignty of the Spirit has changed the way I minister to people in prayer. I took many counseling classes in graduate school. In the early years of my ministry I diligently applied the fruits of my psychological studies to my pastoral counseling appointments. Sometimes the people I counseled were helped; often they left just as stuck as when they came in. This was discouraging for both parishioner and pastor, and for some time I stopped counseling altogether.

When my views began to change regarding how the Spirit touches a believer's life, my approach to counseling began to change as well. Rather than using a counseling approach and strategy gleaned from graduate school, I now begin by simply inviting the Holy Spirit to lead us in our time together. I have no agenda for the time, but try to be very sensitive to what the Spirit wants to do in the person's life that day. Most often the Spirit works quietly to remove the basic barriers that keep us from growing spiritually. He will surface sins that must be confessed, lies that must be renounced and replaced with scriptural truth, or destructive life patterns that can readily be changed by applying basic biblical principles.

Some of our struggles, however, come from much deeper places. Our inner worlds are mysterious, wonderful universes with as much complexity as any stellar galaxy. Wounds received decades earlier are still very much alive in this inner world, and if we have not dealt with them biblically, they fester and bleed and become infected. Our spiritual journey sometimes leads to unhealed places so that we may bring this pain before Christ's healing touch. Typically, however, we are neither fully aware of these internal wounds nor able to call them up at will. Carefully constructed defense mechanisms, meticulously designed to protect us from pain, have kept these secret places far from our conscious mind. When God wants to heal an emotional wound, he begins to get our attention by allowing hints to gurgle up from the deep recesses of our interior.

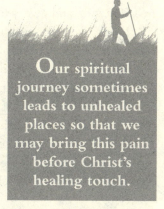

We may encounter anger we did not know we had, lust that is irrational and baseless, or fears that explode to the surface of our conscious mind through the portal of our dream life. Try as we might, we cannot stuff these troubling symptoms beneath the surface where they belong. Our defense mechanisms work overtime to keep them hidden.

Our spiritual journey sometimes leads to unhealed places so that we may bring this pain before Christ's healing touch.

How can we dismantle these protective devices long enough to let us get a good look at what is beneath? How do we access these inner mysteries and bring them out into Christ's healing light? Special touches of the Holy Spirit help us break through spiritual barriers. Time and time again I have watched in amazement as the wonderful Counselor overcomes the defense mechanisms of the mind and sets free the captive emotions hidden beneath consciousness.

Sometimes the gift of spiritual language is released, and pent-up, painful emotions that have been buried for years come pouring out. Other times the Spirit gives a gentle vision that describes the broken inner world better than words ever could. Emotions that have never been felt—but must be felt to be forgiven and healed—spring forth. Occasionally the person being prayed for will rest in the Spirit—a relaxed but conscious state that loosens the protective chains that bind painful memories—and release these memories for healing prayer.

The Holy Spirit is a creative Spirit, and he often uses our imagination to renew our inner worlds. Theresa went to a conference where a gifted counselor was speaking on healing prayer. When she began to speak about fear, Theresa sensed that God had something for her that day.

"She told us to imagine that our inner world was like a garden," Theresa remembers. "We prayed that God would show us the weeds of our garden. I was surprised to find a giant tree right in the center of my garden."

The speaker leading the prayer time said, "Some of you may see a tree. Pull it up and give it to the Father."

Theresa sensed that the tree represented fear. She asked God to remove it. "I felt a sensation of the tree being pulled, leaving a gaping hole. A prayer counselor laid hands on me, and the hole from the tree was filled with soil. I felt lightheaded, euphoric. God healed something in me that had been hurt as a young child. Looking back, I see that that healing prayer was the beginning of a journey for me. I came away with an awareness of some things I'd never known before."

The special touch of the Spirit brought healing to Theresa's life, drawing forth and cleansing a childhood wound she had not known was there.

WILL WE EMBRACE THE "WITH US GOD"?

Jesus Christ is Emmanuel, the God who is with us. The Savior who has drawn near. Yet how near will we let him get? Will we embrace a God who draws near enough to touch us? For many, the answer is no.

In her book *Teaching a Stone to Talk*, Annie Dillard describes a frustrating church service during Advent, the season on the church calendar set aside to reflect on the Withness of God.

> It is the second Sunday in Advent. . . . No one, least of all the organist, could find the opening hymn. Then no one knew it. Then no one could sing it anyways. . . .
>
> > Holy, Holy, Holy Lord,
> > God of Power and Might,
> > Heaven and earth are full of your glor . . .
>
> Does anyone have the foggiest idea what sort of power we so blithely invoke? Or, as I suspect, does no one believe a word of it? . . . It is madness to wear ladies' straw hats and velvet hats to church; we should all be wearing crash helmets. Ushers should issue life preservers and signal flares; they should lash us to our pews. For the sleeping god may wake someday and take offence, or the waking god may draw us out to where we can never return.[17]

TWELVE

INTIMACY AND THE BIRTH OF VISION

I lay on my daughter's bed the other night and looked into blue eyes that could have been my own. My eyes stayed fixed on hers as we discussed the nuances of middle-school life, but my thoughts slipped away to the rainy July afternoon a dozen years ago when we brought her home from the hospital. "Why is everyone trying to hit us?" I had asked Sandi, cautiously turning our 1981 Citation into the Burger King lot like a sophomore in his first day of driver's ed. "They're not," she grinned. "You're just nervous."

I was nervous. I was also in awe. I had just witnessed the birth of a child—my child—and I am still not over it. The birth of each of our children was to me a sacred mystery. Their grand entrances into the world never became routine for us. In fact, I was so excited when our last child was born that I patiently set up the video camera on its tripod to capture the event for eternity—and then proceeded to stand in front of the camera for the entire birth.

The fruit of intimate union in marriage is usually the birth of children. Conception results from intimate communion. The earliest pages of the Bible reveal that sexual union is at the heart of God's redemptive strategy for the world. "Male and female he created them," we read. Then God blesses the couple and says, "Be fruitful and increase in number; fill the earth and subdue it."[1]

Spiritual intimacy with Christ is also deeply satisfying. Yet intimate spirituality is not an end in itself. God has ordained that we "know" him intimately, that we become spiritually fruitful and multiply his kingdom around the earth. When we know God intimately, he impregnates us with vision—a picture of what he wants to do in and through our lives. The fruit of intimate union with Christ is birth—the conception of God's vision for our lives.

We began this book wondering if a relationship with Christ could touch our deepest needs. It can, does, and will. This may be a wise question to begin a book with, but it is not the final question that must be asked. The Son of God does not exist to meet our needs. We exist to meet his. He calls us to know him so intimately that he might impregnate us with fresh vision and further his kingdom on earth through us.

THE LOSS OF A VISION

Few men have been more destined for greatness than Meriwether Lewis. The brilliant American explorer whose leadership of the famous Lewis and Clark expedition to the Pacific and back ranks with Columbus, Magellan, and Cook as one of the world's greatest adventurers. The son of a Virginian gentleman farmer, Lewis joined the Virginia militia during the Whiskey Rebellion and quickly rose through the ranks, earning a reputation as a man who knew the wilderness and the Indians who inhabited it as well as anyone could. When a fellow Virginian named Thomas Jefferson, newly inaugurated as the third president of the United States, invited him to become his personal assistant, Captain Lewis accepted and found himself swept up in one of the most electrifying moments of American history.

Jefferson had a vision of one great nation spreading from coast to coast. He abhorred the thought of his precious continent being chopped up into warring nation-states as Europe had been. Concerned about advances from the French and Spanish, the president saw the need to explore the West and claim it for the United States. Even more important, he wanted to find a water passage linking the Atlantic with the Pacific. Lewis seemed uniquely fitted to lead such a dangerous journey, and Jefferson prepared him for the task by connecting him with key political and military figures in Washington and by apprenticing him with the nation's leading scientists.

Broad-shouldered, well-built, and over six feet tall, Lewis epitomized the Enlightenment optimism that pervaded Jefferson's presidency. At 3:30 P.M. on May 21, 1804, amid cheers from a crowd on the river bank, Lewis, Captain William Clark, and a party of two dozen soldiers set off up the Missouri River, cutting themselves off from civilization for the next three and a half years. Only one soldier would not return.

Lewis soon proved that Jefferson had chosen wisely. A gifted writer, he recorded in detailed journals the discovery of 178 new plants and 122 new species of animals. Adept at navigating the mysterious culture of the Indians, he crossed thousands of miles of hostile territory while hardly firing a bullet in self-defense. Respected by their troops, he and Clark began their lifelong friendship. They worked together to keep their team motivated and disciplined through subzero winters, near-starvation, and sickness.

Eight thousand miles and twenty-eight months after they began, Lewis and his men finally arrived back in St. Louis on September 22, 1806. He had successfully led one of history's most daring expeditions—and instantly became a national celebrity. "He was the fittest person in the world for such an expedition," Jefferson wrote of his young protégé. Filled with thrilling tales of grizzlies and fierce Indians, Lewis became the darling of Washington, cruising from one party to the next, drinking in toast after toast to "the brave captain" who had achieved what no one had accomplished before him.

Jefferson appointed Lewis governor of the Louisiana Territory shortly after his return. History shows this was a tragic mistake. The unique gifts and skills that made Lewis a brilliant explorer worked against him in his new role as politician and businessman. Frustrated with a new calling that was so different from the one of his passions, and lacking a compelling vision for the future, Lewis became depressed and began to drink heavily.

The man who navigated half a continent with barely a mistake seemed to have no idea how to make his way through the political obstacles he now confronted on every side. He became increasingly in debt, made no progress in publishing his much anticipated journals, and fared poorly in a perpetual conflict with an angry subordinate. Worst of all, Lewis simply had no reason to live. The purpose for his life had ended when he had achieved his mission. Drained of motivation, he was unable even to begin the critical task of publishing his treasured journals. The fall of 1809 found Governor Lewis slipping ever deeper into despair. As autumn gave way to winter, the great soldier began one final voyage to see his beloved mentor Jefferson. He never got there.

Late in the afternoon of October 9, Governor Lewis arrived at Grinder's Inn, seventy miles west of Nashville, deeply depressed and probably drunk. Early in the morning of October 11 he pulled out a pistol and shot himself in the head. The bullet missed. Lewis rose, shot himself once more in the chest, but failed again to end his life. When the sun rose, Mrs. Grinder's children found the captain cutting himself with a razor. A few moments later, he died. He was thirty-five years old.

> The great quest Meriwether Lewis had spent much of his life preparing for was over, and he had no new vision to put in its place.

Today Meriwether Lewis is buried along the Natchez Trace River near the old site of Grinder's Inn. His grave is marked by a broken shaft, put there by the Tennessee legislature in 1849 as a symbol of "the violent and untimely end of a bright and glorious career."[2]

Meriwether Lewis had lost his vision. The great quest he had spent much of his life preparing for was over, and he had no new vision to put in its place. Stripped of the driving purpose that made his life worth living, one of America's greatest heroes chose premature death over a visionless life.

THE HIGH COST OF A VISIONLESS LIFE

"Deep in our hearts, we all want to find and fulfill a purpose bigger than ourselves," observes Os Guiness. "Only such a larger purpose can inspire us to heights we know we could never reach on our own. For each of us the real purpose is personal and passionate: to know what we are here to do, and why."[3]

Meriwether Lewis's failure to find a compelling vision for the second half of his life drove him into a black depression, a gnawing psychic pain that the stiffest whiskey could not numb. Many of us respond to the void of personal vision in similar ways. I am convinced that much nonchemically based depression stems from the failure to answer life's most critical questions: Why am I here, and where am I going? The pain of visionless living is so great, we medicate ourselves just as Lewis did. We drink too much, eat too much, click to a pornographic Web site after the kids are in bed, or take a shopping spree to the mall and let Visa pick up the tab.

No one is exempt from the crisis of personal vision.

Teenagers feel it as the world of freedom beyond home and secondary school beckons with a dizzying range of choices.

Graduate students confront it when the excitement of "the world is my oyster" is chilled by the thought that opening up one choice means closing down others.

Those in their early thirties know it when their daily work assumes its own brute reality beyond their earlier considerations of the wishes of their parents, the fashions of their peers, and the allure of salary and career prospects.

People in midlife face it when a mismatch between their gifts and their work reminds them daily that they are square pegs in round holes. Can they see themselves "doing that for the rest of their lives"?

Mothers feel it when their children grow up, and they wonder which high purpose will fill the void in the next stage of life.

People in their forties and fifties with enormous success suddenly come up against it when their accomplishments raise questions concerning the social responsibility of their success and, deeper still, the purpose of their lives.

People confront it in all the varying transitions of life—from moving homes to switching jobs to breakdowns in marriage to crises of health. Negotiating the changes feels longer and worse than the changes themselves because transition challenges our sense of personal meaning.

Those in their later years face it again. What does life add up to? Were the successes real, and were they worth the tradeoffs? Having gained the whole world, however huge or tiny, have we sold our souls cheaply and missed the point of it all? As Walker Percy wrote, "You can get all A's and still flunk life."[4]

MY VISION QUEST

The process of writing this book has helped me reflect on my own crisis of vision. For most of my life I have sought personal vision by asking, "Who does my church need me to be?" In my twenties and early thirties I tried to discover personal vision by asking, "What do successful pastors look like?" I would travel to their seminars, read their books, listen to their tapes, and even at times try to dress like them.

Yet the quest for personal vision will never be fulfilled by aping the vision of respected peers or by trying to meet every need that arises around you. Personal vision ultimately comes from one place: intimate communion with God.

For me, a season of quiet reflection followed our Solemn Assembly. For the first time in my life, I felt the freedom to ask the questions, "Who am I really? What do I really love to do? What is my passion, the unique purpose for which I was created?" Simply asking the question this way unleashed remarkable energy in my soul and provided some very rich times of interaction with my never-failing Friend. Our walks together became a very special part of my spiritual life.

> Personal vision ultimately comes from one place: intimate communion with God.

I was fearful at first of truly listening to my heart. This seemed selfish, irresponsible. After all, wasn't I supposed to serve the church regardless of my needs? Eventually Jesus helped me realize that I will serve the church most effectively when I am serving out of the deepest passions of my heart.

Close behind this first fear was a second one: What if I listen to my heart and find I am in the wrong place? Ironically, the church was going through a restructuring process at this time. What if the church decided that its needs for a senior pastor did not intersect with what my heart was calling me to be? I love our church, our city, and our friends, and I have often said that I want to give my life to Knoxville. Yet part of my journey into a renewed personal vision meant facing the real possibility of painful change.

When I came to the place where I could freely listen to my heart, I was surprised to meet the real me. Here is what I found.

> I am a churchman. I love the local church. And I love our local church.
> I am an artist. I paint with words. I am a writer.
> I am an introvert. I need many hours of silence and reflection built into my life.
> I am a visionary. I can see what the future can become.
> I am a preacher. I am never more alive than when I preach.
> I am a teacher. I love to expand a student's mind with a great idea.
> I also discovered who I am not: I am not the CEO of a large nonprofit organization.

Then I noticed something else. When I ministered in my "heart" areas, my life impacted those around me significantly. Serving in these areas left a wake of blessing behind me. When I ministered as a CEO (which was about sixty percent of the time), I hurt those around me, leaving bruised relationships, mistrust, and confusion in my wake.

The walks with Jesus continued. The closer I drew to him, the clearer my personal vision became. Eventually I shared with my elders just what was emerging. These men love me very much and are committed to both the church and to me. They tell the truth and do not pull any punches. We talked frankly about my vision, the church's needs, and where I fit in. Several weeks later, I wrote them the following letter.

Good Friday, 1999

Dear Brothers,
I have spent many hours thinking about the past elder meeting. If I understood you correctly, I heard you say that you affirmed my calling to preach, pray, write, and disciple. . . . I also

heard you say that when I operate outside of the realm of my gifts and calling, I am not effective and make mistakes that often hurt people. You graciously said that this was not my intent, but nonetheless was the reality. Finally, I believe you said that you wanted to create a position for me that allowed me to be who God has called me to be and also released me from doing things I do not do well.

I've pondered this a great deal these past two weeks, and have been surprised at the degree of freedom and hope I have found from considering laying down the reins of organizational leadership and leading more from my other gifts. This makes sense to me, because I have been totally frustrated serving as an "organizational leader" while finding fulfillment leading as a teacher or vision caster. I have been well aware for some time that the church has outgrown my organizational leadership abilities. I cannot describe to you how frustrating it has been to see people continually hurt by my organizational leadership wake.

For a season, I wondered if it was time for me to step down and allow another with stronger gifts in these areas to take my place at the helm. Since then, through a variety of means including your input, I have sensed the Lord encouraging me that there is still an important place for me at Fellowship, but for me to find this place I must be entirely willing to lay down the parts of the ministry I have no calling to fulfill. I have not considered myself to be a power hungry man, but I do see how I have been reluctant to release control to others. . . .

Please allow me to immediately hand off my role as chairman of the elder board. I have served in this capacity for twelve years now. It is time for me to relinquish this role. . . . This process has given me much hope.

Warmly in Christ,
Doug

The hope and freedom I have experienced in ministry since this transition have been remarkable. My joy is returning. I am not continually hurting people anymore. The areas I am working in are increasing in fruitfulness. I actually am having fun!

The past two years of my life have been about two themes: renewed intimacy and renewed vision. The collapse of my addiction to success thrust me into a crisis of faith: Can Jesus satisfy my deepest longings? He can, and he does. As I am coming to know him more intimately, he is impregnating me with fresh vision for the future.

WHAT IS A PERSONAL VISION?

What is a personal vision? It is our life Quest, the reason for which we were created. Our personal vision is our own unique story, our lines in the broader drama God is writing for humanity. Personal vision begins with a general grasp of what God is doing in the world and then moves to the particulars of how we personally will join him in this great work.

"When David had served God's purpose in his own generation, he fell asleep."[5] Each of us is to serve God's purpose in our own generation before we die. Do you know what your unique vision is?

Leighton Ford defines a personal vision as "unexpected, awesome, personal, clear, specific and empowered." A personal vision is unexpected—because God gives it to us. It is awesome—because only God can bring it to pass. It is personal—because it intersects with the longings of our own heart. It is clear and specific—at least in terms of the next steps to take. And if it is to be fulfilled, it must be empowered by the Holy Spirit.[6]

> Personal vision begins with a general grasp of what God is doing in the world and then moves to the particulars of how we personally will join him in this great work.

INTIMACY AND THE BIRTH OF VISION?

Where do such visions come from? They are born out of intimate times of tender communion with our beloved Christ. Spiritual union with Christ gives birth to new vision just as sexual union in marriage gives birth to new life.

Jesus calls us to know him as a man knows his wife.[7] The parallels between sexual union and spiritual union are important to grasp. The husband draws into intimacy with his wife, releasing his seed into her and impregnating her with new life. In a similar way, Christ draws close to us, impregnating us with his vision.

HALF TIME

Jack, a nuclear engineer and devoted member of his local church, was enjoying a rare Saturday afternoon alone in his South Carolina home. A friend had given him the autobiography *From Ashes to Glory,* the gripping story of Coach Bill McCartney's painful spiritual journey that eventually resulted in the birth of the Promise Keepers men's movement.[8] "God's presence suddenly overwhelmed me," Jack remembers. "I cried out to God—'Whatever it takes, Lord! I don't want to miss your perfect will for my life. Whatever it takes!'"

Jack and his family had been devoted to their local church for twelve years. His career as a consultant was steadily on track. But something was about to change, and he knew it.

"I was entering into half time," Jack laughs. "I was about to spend a long season in the locker room looking at tape from the first half of my life and figuring out where to go during the next half."

Bit by bit, Jack slowly reduced his responsibilities at church and began spending more time alone with God. Then his consulting business dried up. "For a year and a half, we got by one little job at a time," he says. Jack sensed this was a time of unusual significance in his life. Fighting everything within him, he chose not to aggressively look for new work. "My number-one priority during that season was to seek God. God had shown me in Ephesians 2:10 that he has a unique plan for each of his children. I kept asking God to show me what my part was in fulfilling his kingdom."

A month went by. Then six months. A year. "Some mornings I woke up in fear," Jack admits. "But I kept on seeking God. I didn't want to leave the locker room until he told me to."

Several more months went by. Funds were running out. Yet Jack continued to follow hard after God. Toward the end of the seventeenth month "in the locker room," Jack stopped asking for the entire game plan for the rest of his life, and he prayed, "Just show me the next step." A few days later, the phone rang. Could he come to work at church for a year and help get things smoothed out operationally? Jack said yes. The second half had begun.

One year turned into two, and now Jack is the director of operations at Fellowship Church. His second-half vision, while not filled out in every detail, is becoming clearer and more personal. "My personal vision is to help create enduring organizations that know God and are led by the Spirit," he tells me, the excitement building in his voice as he utters each phrase. Jack has discovered his purpose on earth for this generation. God birthed this vision in him as he spent intimate time with him.

THE POWER OF THE MOST HIGH WILL OVERSHADOW YOU

I visited the Vatican Museum in Rome on the way home from a missions trip several years ago. Shelling out a few liras for a pair of headphones and a taped tour guide, I set out to explore some of the world's most spectacular art. A few hours into the tour I came across a room filled with paintings dedicated to the veneration of the Virgin Mary. Captions written in many languages explained the Roman Catholic Church's belief that Mary was quite different from the rest of us—and worthy of our adoration and praise.

I cut the rest of the tour short that day, saddened by the subtle message spoken by the beautiful paintings in Mary's special room. The poetic majesty of the Christmas story is not Mary's uniqueness, but her normalness. Young Mary was what we might call a member of the working poor, scraping out a living in a tiny little frontier village on the farthest edge of the Roman Empire. She was engaged to be married to a minimum-wage common laborer who asked for her hand in marriage with sawdust on his robe and splinters in his fingers. And yet God gave birth to the vision through her.

"You've got to be kidding!" Mary stutters to the angelic apparition that had woken her up. And then she feels compelled to state the obvious. "I'm a virgin."

The angel replies, "The Holy Spirit will come upon you, and the power of the Most High will overshadow you. So the holy one to be born will be called the Son of God."[9]

Mary had an empty womb. It held no seed. God placed the seed within her as the Spirit overshadowed her. Out of an intimate communion Scripture does not describe, the Promised Child was conceived. Jewish readers would have immediately understood that "overshadowed" was a Hebrew way of describing being overcome by the presence of the living God. When vision is birthed in Scripture, it is most often conceived in the presence of God. Moses' vision is birthed before the burning bush. Abraham's Quest is conceived in a worship ceremony. Jesus' call to public ministry is graced by the dove descending at his baptism, symbolizing the presence of God the Father.

This is God's way. The Holy Spirit impregnates Mary by covering her with the shadow of his presence. So it is with us. The Spirit impregnates us with vision when we are drawn into the presence of God. One of the Greek words the Bible uses to describe our inner worlds means "womb." In a sense, we are all virgins with empty wombs, waiting for God to impregnate us with vision.

DEEP GLADNESS

Sometimes God rekindles vision in us as we come near him by reminding us of passions long forgotten. Frederick Buechner wisely suggests that our personal vision is "the place where your deep gladness and the world's deep hunger meet."[10] Our deep gladness is often buried, however, beneath layers of life's oughts and shoulds.

> Sometimes God rekindles vision in us as we come near him by reminding us of passions long forgotten.

My wife's deep gladness is worshiping God through dance. One afternoon in a college dance class, Sandi sensed Christ in the room watching her. That intimate moment with her Savior put the seed of a vision in Sandi's heart. "I realized that day that this was the purpose of dance—to worship him."

Sadly, Sandi quickly discovered that the Christians in her world did not celebrate this new vision with her. They discouraged her from taking dance classes and made it clear that the world of dance was no place for a godly woman. She married me and was shocked to find that we had to sign a "no dancing" covenant as part of the seminary's entrance requirements. The vision quietly began to die.

A dozen years passed. Our church began to rediscover the creative arts, and a dance ministry began. Tentatively, Sandi began to dance again. At first it was simply for fun—a great way to spend an evening with friends and express herself in a way she loved. But then the dance ministry matured into a worshiping community that began to experience the gifts and power of the Spirit. The group spent many evenings in worship and prayer for one another without ever moving to the dance floor.

I began to notice a change in Sandi. A pastime was becoming a throbbing passion in her life. Her long-forgotten vision to worship God with dance had come alive again.

"Recently I've had more time to spend with God than in many years," Sandi says. "The more time I spend with him, the more the vision expands." These intimate times have also surfaced feelings of grief and loss. "I lost those years and can never get them back again," she says softly as she considers the period in her life when there was no place for her to pursue her own deep gladness. "The years in my life when I had the physical skills and ability to dance well are gone."

Her vision, however, is not gone. "God is unfolding his vision for me as we spend more and more time together. I really want to see God use dance in the church for his glory. I want to help a younger generation of dancers reclaim this art form and learn to worship God through it."

We began our book with Brian's struggle with Internet pornography. I saw Brian recently and noticed a brightness in his eyes that I had never seen before. I called him to find out where his own Quest had taken him. Brian is a very brave man with an enormous love for God. His commitment to integrity and wholeness was beginning to pay off.

Brian explained that he shared his struggle with his pastor and a few close friends. He began meeting weekly with a Christian counselor and a sexual addiction support group. Slowly, the chains of his addiction are being broken. A wounded heart that had been impervious to emotion for thirty years is beginning to mend; and Brian is beginning to bond with his wife, his father, and his God.

Our conversation ended by Brian commenting that he was starting to think again about God's calling on his life. He was beginning to see that his own struggle could one day help others enter wholeness. Brian has paid the price by pursuing intimacy with Christ over the lesser gods of his lusts. And Christ is rewarding him with a new life vision.

I have chosen Brian's story to end our journey together because it captures my hope for everyone who reads this book. All of us are addicts. Each of us is born with a bent heart and a stubborn determination to drink from any cup other than the holy grail of intimacy with Christ. Like Brian, each of us must flee the high places of our addictions and nail our deepest desires to Jesus. But the story does not—and must not—end with our personal fulfillment. The Fisher King languished in his barren kingdom, nursing a wound that never healed, awaiting the day someone would drink from the Grail and set him free. When we begin to drink from the grail of intimate communion with Christ, he impregnates us with vision for the wounded kings and queens who inhabit barren kingdoms all around us.

I have been writing this book now for nearly two years. I have learned much about the Quest. Yet, as I reread the opening chapters in a search of the appropriate way to say goodbye to you, I am saddened by the parts of my heart that remain untouched by all that we thought about together. Let me give you an example.

This morning I left the cabin where I write and took a walk around a mountain lake. Writing a book is like climbing a mountain. The work is always hardest near the summit. Finishing a book is much harder than beginning one. Yet this time I found a residue of resentment settling over me, a joylessness in the task of writing that I had not felt before. Peering through the clear, gray waters of the lake, I saw a submerged tree creating ripples on the otherwise still surface above it. "Father," I prayed. "Show me what is beneath the surface of my heart. Why is there so little joy as I reach the end of this two-year journey?"

Gradually God let me see what was submerged beneath the lake of my conscious mind. I found that the old longing for applause had crept in again. The need to succeed, to be somebody, to make a name for myself had entangled itself with the genuine desires that prompted me to write this book. Now that it was ready to be presented to the world, would anybody care? Would the fathers clap? Would I become a noted expert on spiritual intimacy and abruptly be asked to speak at conferences, or perhaps be invited to be the key speaker on a Christian cruise or a tour through the Holy Land?

Now I saw the submerged tree. It was the rotten stump of a belief that writing a book will satisfy my deepest need to be somebody special. The unlikelihood of this happening threatened my sense of self. And so I was having a hard time finishing the book.

I have taken the risk of sharing my own struggles with you, my friend, because I suspect that when you take your own walk around the lake of your heart you, too, will find a submerged tree or two. Do not give up. I will not quit if you will not. Let's pray for one another that the words of the apostle Paul might become our own:

> All the things I once thought were so important are gone from my life. Compared to the high privilege of knowing Christ Jesus as my Master, firsthand, everything I once thought I had going for me is insignificant—dog dung. I have dumped it all in the trash so that I could embrace Christ and be embraced by him. . . .
>
> I gave up all that inferior stuff so I could know Christ personally, experience his resurrection power, be a partner in his suffering, and go all the way with him to death itself.[11]

AFTERTHOUGHTS

Reflections on Sexuality and Spirituality

ot one!" the police officer exclaimed, sounding like a fisherman who had just hooked a five-pound bass. I was spending the evening in his patrol car on a pastoral "ride along" and was about to experience my first "bust." Blue lights flashing, he ripped his car into a 180-degree turn and floored it in hot pursuit of the criminal.

"What's he done?" I asked, spilling my coffee and hoping we hadn't just found an armed robber.

"See that girl?" he asked, pointing at a woman in a flimsy summer dress disappearing into the shadows behind a liquor store. "She's a prostitute. She just got out of that guy's car. This street's a real hot spot for prostitution. You can even find a map of it on the Internet."

The car we were chasing, a new sports utility vehicle, pulled to the curb. The officer got out and invited me to join him. *What kind of man is out looking for prostitutes at 11:30 on a Sunday night?* I wondered. A pretty normal man, I soon found out. The "criminal" nervously reached for his driver's license as the officer's high-powered flashlight searched his car. A baby's car seat was in the back, surrounded by a few children's toys. Recently dry-cleaned laundry hung on a hanger, just as it often does in my car. Fear and shame covered the man's face.

"You're not going to take me in, are you? Please, don't!" he pleaded.

The officer chose to have mercy and warned the man to "get back home to your wife."

What *was* this man looking for at 11:30 on a Sunday night? Why are we so driven by our sexual passions? Sexual longing is one of the most powerful forces in the universe. A president throws away his legacy for a moment of sexual gratification with a young intern. A pastor wipes out a lifetime of ministry for a fleeting moment of oneness with a woman he is counseling. A lonely coed says yes to her boyfriend's demand for sex when everything in her screams no! A father of three slips away, after tucking his children into bed, for a thirty-dollar tryst with a prostitute.

Have you ever wondered why? Why are men and women so drawn to unite sexually? What is the source of this raw power that topples empires, wrecks ministries, and shatters families? What are we looking for in sex, anyway?

THE BEAUTY OF THE FEMININE

I have often been puzzled by my own strong attraction to feminine beauty. I am deeply in love with my wife, have a disciplined thought life, and don't expose myself to pornography. Yet I find within me an ever-present attraction to the beauty of the feminine. By God's grace and power, I have yielded these desires to the Spirit's control and joyfully find these longings fulfilled in my relationship with Sandi.

But why won't these feelings and desires simply go away? Why do I have to fight them at all? Is something wrong with me?

Once, in a counseling session, I shared these questions with my counselor.

"Have you ever thought you might be looking for God?" he asked.

"God is masculine," I replied. "I'm drawn to the feminine." It just didn't add up.

Since then, I have discovered in a new way that feminine beauty, like all beauty, flows out of the character of God. God does exhibit masculine traits in the Bible, and we are told to call him Father. But he is not merely masculine. "God created man in his own image," we read in the first pages of the creation account. "In the image of God he created him; male and female he created them."[1]

Men and women together reflect the image of God, so there must be *both* masculinity and femininity in God's character. "Our Creator," comments Leanne Payne, "holding all that is true and real within himself, reflects both the masculine and the feminine."[2] The God of the Scriptures demonstrates many so-called masculine traits. Indeed, Jesus teaches us to pray to "our Father in heaven."[3] God exemplifies many of the characteristics we associate with maleness: He is a warrior and a problem solver, he is rational and principled, and he expresses himself through clear objective truth.

This same God, however, is more than merely masculine. As the One who is the ground of all being, he contains within himself all that is feminine as well. We are not surprised to see so-called feminine traits in him. He is a nurturer, a comforter, and a healer. He promises Israel, "As a mother comforts her child, so will I comfort you."[4] He can be intuitive and subjective, and he is as concerned for relationship as he is for truth. God, who is beyond sexuality, contains all that is masculine and feminine within himself.

This means that feminine beauty reflects a unique dimension of the beauty of God. The yearning to be intimate with, to be consumed by the feminine is at the core a yearning to taste the aspects of God that are reflected in pure femininity.

LISTENING TO THE WHISPERS OF SEXUAL DESIRE

This divine femininity began to make sense to me when I began looking at what was going on in my life when sexual longings were the strongest. Typically these were times when I was under stress or very fatigued and in need of nurture and comfort. I am learning to listen to the sexual yearnings of my heart, because they are telling me that my soul is searching for something much deeper—an intimate encounter with God.

Jesus linked spiritual oneness with sexual oneness when he chose the Greek word for sexual intercourse when speaking of knowing God.[5] Could it be that God intended for our sexual longings to remind us of our ache for him? Frederick Buechner has written that "beneath the longing to possess and be possessed by another sexually—to know in the biblical idiom—there lies the longing to know and be known . . . to be at long last where you fully belong."[6]

I am no longer ashamed of my sexuality. I accept these longings as an invitation to know God more intimately. Stripped of their mystery, sexual urges become a gift, a whisper from within, inviting me to slow down and take a look at my heart.

Sexual longing is ultimately a thirst for transcendence, a quest for oneness and communion with God. Sexuality and spirituality are closely related; one mirrors the other. Our obsession with sexual union masks a deeper, spiritual obsession to reconnect with God. "Just as we experience deep joy as we lose ourselves and merge into oneness with our spouse," writes Dan Allender, "we experience ultimate joy as we become one with Jesus Christ in a union that leads to incomprehensible joy. Marital intercourse mirrors our relationship to God."[7]

EXPLORING THE RIDDLE OF SEXUALITY AND SPIRITUALITY

The Song of Songs explores the riddle of sexuality and spirituality through a romantic Hebrew poem. While interpretations of the poem differ, many agree that the Song on one level compares sexual intimacy with spiritual intimacy. The mystic Bernard of Clairvaux drew upon the Song for teaching on spiritual intimacy in the twelfth century. Old Testament scholar Tremper Longman draws the same lessons from it in the twentieth century.[8] Let's consider what the poem might teach us about intimate spirituality. Hopefully, some of the tension we feel between sexuality and spirituality will be resolved as we do.[9]

CONVERSATION

The first stage in intimate prayer is conversation. Wise lovers know that genuine intimacy begins with tender, unhurried conversation. There must be pursuit. There must be connection. The lovers "get to know each other again" after a busy day. Concerns are shared. Wounds are dressed. Words of affirmation and hope are spoken. We find the lovers in the Song of Songs beginning with conversation:

"How beautiful you are, my darling!" says the groom.

"How handsome you are, my lover!" answers the bride.[10]

Intimate prayer also must begin with tender conversation. We can rush into God's presence no more successfully than we can rush into the bedroom. We must take time to "get to know God again" when a busy day has passed since we last met. This first stage is a time of reviving our ongoing dialogue with our Lord. We read the Word as a primary means of initiating this dialogue. Journaling and worship also facilitate the journey to intimacy at this stage. Anticipation heightens as we long for greater closeness.

ONENESS

Lovers who have taken the time to reconnect their souls and carry the burdens of one another's hearts ease toward sexual oneness. Communication becomes nonverbal, less rational. Emotions are stirred.

The wife in the Song of Songs, filled with longing after the intimate talk she has shared with her lover, invites him to become one with her:

> Awake, north wind,
> and come, south wind!
> Blow on my garden,
> that its fragrance may spread abroad.
> Let my lover come into his garden
> and taste its choice fruits.

The lover celebrates their union:

> I have come into my garden, my sister, my bride;
> I have gathered my myrrh with my spice.
> I have eaten my honeycomb and my honey;
> I have drunk my wine and my milk.

The chorus celebrates with them:

> Eat, O friends, and drink;
> drink your fill, O lovers.[11]

The line between sexuality and spirituality is a thin one. The lover and the beloved become one, their sexual longing illuminating an ache for spiritual oneness. "Of all the sensations we can experience with our physical senses," writes Mike Mason, reflecting on the sacramental nature of sexual intercourse, "surely this is the one that comes closest to the

Lord's Supper in being an actual touching of the source of our being, of our Creator."[12]

What happens in the oneness phase of intimate prayer? We find joy, fulfillment, release, closeness, and a warmth that transcends reason. There is security, belonging, and at times, rapture.

REST

The time immediately after sexual union is precious for most couples. All is quiet. There are no words, just the delicious presence of one another, the mysterious sense of two hearts beating as one. It is not a time for planning or asking or talking, only rest.

After the Lover and the Beloved in the Song of Songs celebrate their union, they rest.

"I slept, but my heart was awake," the Beloved says.[13]

This is the time I enjoy more than any other in intimate prayer. I spend a day each week fasting and praying and studying the Scripture. The hard work of intercession is behind me. I have received whatever word Christ has for me that day. Weather permitting, I end the day by walking to a nearby dock and lying down by the water's edge. As the river breeze rushes over me, I am tangibly aware of the presence of God. I ask for nothing. God says nothing. We are simply one in spirit.

IMPREGNATION

The most visible fruit of sexual union is a child. When a husband and wife are one, the wife is impregnated with the seed of the man, and new life is conceived. In the same way, vision is birthed out of our times of intimate oneness with Christ. The Beloved in the Song of Songs is reborn with a fresh desire to run with her Lover and serve in his vineyards:

> I belong to my lover,
>> and his desire is for me.
> Come, my lover, let us go to the countryside,
>> let us spend the night in the villages.
> Let us go early to the vineyards

to see if the vines have budded,
if their blossoms have opened,
   and if the pomegranates are in bloom—
   there I will give you my love.[14]

Likewise, when we draw close to Christ, we are ignited with fresh vision and a deeper passion to serve him. We, too, will rise early to look for fruit in the vineyard of our ministries. Intimacy with Christ births vision for Christ. God impregnates us with vision as we are intimate with him.

THE GIFT OF SEXUAL DESIRE

Sadly, our sexuality often drives us away from God instead of toward him. Ashamed of our longings and desires, we see our sexuality as a demon needing exorcism. Sexual longing is not a demon. It is a beautiful part of who we are as people made in the image of Christ. Listen to the whispers of your own sexual desires. You won't find a demon. You just might find God.

NOTES

Prologue

1. J. R. R. Tolkien, *The Hobbit* (New York: Ballantine Books, 1966), 16.
2. Ibid., 28.
3. Ibid., 302.

Chapter 1: When We Fail to Bond with God

1. The names and some of the details in many stories in this book have been changed to protect confidentiality.
2. John 17:21.
3. Genesis 1:26, emphasis added.
4. Genesis 2:18.
5. Dr. Henry Cloud, *Changes That Heal* (Grand Rapids: Zondervan, 1992), 49. The thoughts on bonding in this chapter come primarily from his book.
6. Ibid., 55.
7. John 15:1–6 *The Message*.
8. Jeremiah 2:13.
9. Gerald May, *Addiction and Grace* (New York: Harper & Row, 1988), 9, 11.
10. Ibid., 3.
11. Chemical imbalances in our bodies can cause severe depression, and it is always a good idea to visit a physician when we are depressed.
12. Galatians 5:16–22.
13. Isaiah 1:13–14.
14. Matthew 23:4.
15. Revelation 3:16.
16. Leonard Sweet, *SoulTsunami: Sink or Swim in New Millennium Culture* (Grand Rapids: Zondervan, 1999), 19.
17. John 15:6.
18. For readers wanting to learn more about this particular struggle, known as transference, I highly recommend Valerie McIntyre's book, *Sheep in Wolves Clothing: How Unseen Need Destroys Friendship and Community and What to Do About It* (Grand Rapids: Baker, 1999).

19. Matthew 22:37–39.

Chapter 2: My Journey Beyond Addiction

1. C. S. Lewis, "The Inner Ring," Commemorative Oration at King's College, University of London, 1944.

2. Gerald May, *Addiction and Grace* (New York: Harper & Row, 1988), 1, 3.

3. God is always the initiator in our spiritual lives. We are always the responders. In this sense, God holds the masculine role, and every Christian—both men and women—the feminine.

4. Lewis, "The Inner Ring."

5. Psalm 16:6.

6. Romans 5:5; 6:5; 8:14, 26.

7. May, *Addiction and* Grace, 13.

8. Ezekiel 14:6.

9. Ezekiel 16:26

10. 2 Kings 18:1–5.

11. This practice is identified in Joel 1:14.

12. 2 Corinthians 7:9.

13. May, *Addiction and Grace*, 11.

Chapter 3: As Christ Loved the Church

1. Isaiah 54:4–8; Jeremiah 2:2–3; Hosea 1–3; see also Isaiah 5:1–7.

2. Ephesians 5:22–33.

3. Cited in Leanne Payne, *Crisis in Masculinity* (Grand Rapids: Baker, 1995), 87.

4. Ibid., 69.

5. John 15:15.

6. Leslie Weatherhead, *The Transforming Friendship* (Nashville: Abingdon, 1977), 18.

7. Dan B. Allender and Tremper Longman III, *Intimate Allies* (Wheaton, IL: Tyndale House, 1997), 213.

8. Mike Mason, *The Mystery of Marriage* (Portland, OR: Multnomah Press, 1985), 71.

9. 1 Corinthians 6:17.

10. John R. W. Stott, *Life in Christ* (Wheaton, IL: Tyndale House, 1991), 38.

11. Charles Kraft, *Christianity with Power* (Ann Arbor, MI: Servant, 1989), 26.

12. Matthew 12:28.

13. Luke 10:9.

14. Galatians 2:20.

15. 2 Timothy 4:7.

16. See Eugene Peterson, *A Long Obedience in the Same Direction* (Downers Grove, IL: InterVarsity Press, 1980).

Chapter 4: Hearing the Voice of a Dancing Father

1. Matthew 4:4.

2. John 10:27.

3. Revelation 19:13.

4. Robert Bly, *Iron John* (New York: Vintage, 1992), 251.

5. Matthew 3:17.

6. Joshua 3:9.

7. Luke 24:27, emphasis added.

8. Madame Guyon, *Experiencing the Depths of Christ*, Library of Spiritual Classics, vol. 2 (Auburn, ME: Christian Books, 1975), 8.

9. Genesis 24:63.

10. Psalm 63:6.

11. Luke 2:19.

12. Thomas Merton, *Opening the Bible* (Collegeville, MN: Liturgical Press, 1970), 33.

Chapter 5: Prophetic Whispers

1. 1 Timothy 1:18.

2. 1 Corinthians 14:3.

3. Doug Banister, *The Word and Power Church* (Grand Rapids: Zondervan, 1999), 21.

4. 1 Corinthians 14:24–25.

5. Gordon Fee, *The First Epistle to the Corinthians,* New International Commentary on the New Testament (Grand Rapids: Eerdmans, 1987), 686.

6. A. W. Tozer, *The Pursuit of God* (Camp Hill, PA: Christian Publications, 1982), 81–82.

7. John 16:13, 15.

8. John 5:17–20. Jesus worked where the Father was already at work. This is how I try to discern ministry opportunities as well.

9. Numbers 11:29.

10. Joel 2:28–29.

11. Mike Bickle, *Growing in the Prophetic* (Lake Mary, FL: Creation House, 1996).

12. Acts 13:1.

13. Acts 13:2.

14. Acts 8:29.

15. Acts 9:3–6.

16. Acts 9:10.

17. Acts 10:9–13.

18. Acts 11:28.

19. Acts 13:2.

20. Acts 16:6.

21. Acts 16:9–10.

22. Acts 18:9–10.

23. Acts 19:6.

24. Acts 20:22–23.

25. Acts 21:9.

26. Acts 21:10–11.

27. Acts 23:11.

28. Acts 1:1, emphasis added.

29. Acts 2:43.

30. 1 Thessalonians 5:20.

31. George Mallone, *Those Controversial Gifts* (Arlington, TX: Grace Vineyard of Arlington, 1988), 42.

32. Revelation 19:10.

33. Matthew 7:15–20.

34. 1 Corinthians 13:2.

35. Ken Gire, *Windows of the Soul* (Grand Rapids: Zondervan, 1996), 151.

36. Psalm 16:7.

Chapter 6: Prayer and Being Fathered

1. George Buttrick: quoted in Richard Foster, ed., *Devotional Classics* (San Francisco: HarperCollins, 1989), 100.

2. Susan Howatch, *Glittering Images* (New York: Fawcett Crest, 1987), 228, 243.

3. Matthew 6:9.

4. Luke 11:11–13.

5. John Piper, *Let the Nations Be Glad* (Grand Rapids: Baker, 1993), 41.

6. Dallas Willard, *The Divine Conspiracy* (San Francisco: HarperCollins, 1998), 243.

7. Quoted in Elisabeth Elliot, *Through Gates of Splendor* (New York: Harper, 1957), 235–36.

8. Cited in Gordon Dalbey, *Healing the Masculine Soul* (Waco, TX: Word, 1988), 13.

9. Ephesians 6:19.

10. Howatch, *Glittering Images*, 200.

Chapter 7: Shared Intimacies

1. Romans 5:5.

2. Romans 8:14–16.

3. Rudolf Otto, *The Idea of the Holy,* 2d ed. (London: Oxford Press, 1950), 12, 30.

4. 1 Corinthians 14:15.

5. Readers wanting a more detailed exegetical study of 1 Corinthians 14 as the basis for private prayer language may want to read Appendix 2 in my earlier book, *The Word and Power Church.*

6. 1 Corinthians 14:2.

7. 1 Corinthians 12:10.

8. 1 Corinthians 14:2 *The Message.*

9. 1 Corinthians 14:4 *The Message.*

10. 1 Corinthians 14:5.

11. 1 Corinthians 14:18 *The Message.*

12. 1 Corinthians 14:39.

13. Mark 16:17.

14. Gordon Fee, *God's Empowering Presence* (Peabody, MA: Hendrickson, 1994), 585.

15. Romans 8:26.

16. George Mallone, *Those Controversial Gifts* (Arlington, TX: Grace Vineyard of Arlington, 1988), 94.

17. Ephesians 6:12.

18. Ephesians 6:18.

19. Fee, *God's Empowering Presence*, 731.

20. 1 Corinthians 12:10.

21. 1 Corinthians 14:13.

22. 1 Corinthians 14:5.

23. Lucille Nicolisi, Elizabeth Harryman, and Janet Kresheck, *Terminology of Communication Disorders* (Baltimore: Williams and Wilkins, 1978), 98.

24. Jackie Pullinger, *Chasing the Dragon* (Ann Arbor, MI: Servant, 1980), 128.

25. 1 Corinthians 14:15.

26. Colossians 3:16.

27. Derek Prince, *Blessing or Curse: You Can Choose* (Grand Rapids: Chosen Books, 1990), 32.

28. 1 Corinthians 14:23.

29. J. R. R. Tolkien, *The Lord of the Rings* (New York: Ballantine, 1982), 281.

30. 1 Corinthians 12:30 NASB.

31. 1 Corinthians 14:5.

32. 1 Corinthians 12:11.

33. 1 Corinthians 14:1.

Chapter 8: The Fellowship of His Sufferings

1. Habakkuk 1:3.

2. Jeremiah 12:1.

3. Psalm 74:10–11.

4. Psalm 44:24.

5. Philip Yancey, *Disappointment with God* (Grand Rapids: Zondervan, 1988), 23.

6. Parker Palmer, *The Courage to Teach* (San Francisco, CA: Jossey-Bass, 1998), 63.

7. Ibid.

8. C. S. Lewis, *A Grief Observed* (Toronto: Bantam Books, 1988), 4.

9. Habakkuk 3:17–18.

10. Job 42:5.

11. Genesis 50:20.

12. Acts 2:23.

13. Romans 8:28.

14. Read more on this in the next chapter.

15. John Wimber, "Signs, Wonders and Cancer," *Christianity Today* (October 7, 1996): 49–51.

Chapter 9: Rescued

1. Georg Fohrer, "Save," *Theological Dictionary of the New Testament*, ed. Gerald Friedrich, vol. 7 (Grand Rapids: Eerdmans, 1971), 973.
2. Oscar Cullman, *Christ and Time* (Philadelphia: Westminster, 1964), 37ff.
3. John 12:31; 14:30; 16:11.
4. 1 John 5:19.
5. 2 Corinthians 4:4.
6. 1 John 3:8; Luke 4:18.
7. James Kallas, *The Significance of the Synoptic Miracles* (London: SPCK, 1961), 79.
8. Luke 13:16.
9. Acts 10:38.
10. Psalm 103:2–3.
11. Matthew 14:13.
12. Matthew 14:14.
13. Matthew 9:35–36.
14. Luke 4:39.
15. David Seamands, *Healing Damaged Emotions* (Colorado Springs: Chariot Victor, 1991), 11–12.

Chapter 10: Finishing the Quest

1. See third stanza of "Come, Thou Fount" by Robert Robinson.
2. Rosemary Sutcliff, *The Light Beyond the Forest* (New York: Puffin, 1994), 140–41.
3. Eugene Peterson, *A Long Obedience in the Same Direction* (Downers Grove, IL: InterVarsity Press, 1980), 12–13.
4. Sutcliff, *Light Beyond the Forest*, 46, 131.
5. 1 Timothy 1:19.
6. Hebrews 3:12.
7. Leonard Sweet, *SoulTsunami: Sink or Swim in New Millennium Culture* (Grand Rapids: Zondervan, 1999), 77.
8. These statistics, along with many helpful insights about the nature of change in a postmodern culture, are found in Leonard Sweet's excellent postmodern primer, *SoulTsunami*, 71–103.
9. Stephen Ambrose, *Undaunted Courage: Meriwether Lewis, Thomas Jefferson, and the Opening of the American West* (New York: Simon & Schuster, 1997), 325.
10. William Law, *A Serious Call to a Devout and Holy Life* (Philadelphia: Westminster, 1950), 22.
11. Sutcliff, *Light Beyond the* Forest, 44–45.
12. 1 Timothy 4:7.
13. James 5:16.

14. 1 John 1:9.

15. Frederick Buechner, *Telling the Truth* (San Francisco: Harper, 1977), 81–85.

16. See the Mitford series of five novels by Jan Karon, the fifth being *A New Song* (New York: Viking Penguin, 2000).

17. Tom Wolfe, *A Man in Full: A Novel* (New York: Bantam, 1999).

18. Susan Howatch, *Glittering Images* (New York: Fawcett Crest, 1987), 434.

Chapter 11: Special Moments

1. Ian Murray, *Jonathan Edwards: A New Biography* (Carlisle, PA: Banner of Truth, 1988), 42–43, 135.

2. Ibid., 441.

3. Quoted in D. Martyn Lloyd-Jones, *Joy Unspeakable* (Wheaton, IL: Harold Shaw, 1984), 79–80.

4. Blaise Pascal, *Pensées*, trans. A. Krailsheimer (London: Penguin, 1966), 309.

5. Simon Tugwell, ed., *Albert and Thomas, Selected Writings* (New York: Paulist Press, 1988), 266.

6. Cited in Lloyd-Jones, *Joy Unspeakable*, 95–96.

7. Romans 8:15–16.

8. Lloyd-Jones, *Joy Unspeakable*, 95.

9. Ibid., 85.

10. Ibid., 73.

11. Matthew 3:16–17.

12. Numbers 11:25.

13. 1 Samuel 10:10.

14. Acts 10:44–47.

15. Acts 19:6.

16. 1 Corinthians 12:11.

17. Annie Dillard, *Teaching a Stone to Talk* (New York: HarperCollins, 1988), 37, 58.

Chapter 12: Intimacy and the Birth of Vision

1. Genesis 1:27–28.

2. The full story of Lewis's life can be found in the exceptionally well-written book by Stephen Ambrose, *Undaunted Courage: Meriwether Lewis, Thomas Jefferson, and the Opening of the American West* (New York: Simon & Schuster, 1997).

3. Os Guiness, *The Call* (Nashville: Word, 1998), 3.

4. Quoted in Guiness, *The Call*, 2–3.

5. Acts 13:36.

6. To fully understand my thoughts about our intimacy with God and the birth of a vision—which is based on the riddle between sexuality and spirituality as found in the Hebrew poetry of the Old Testament book the Song of Solomon—please read "Afterthoughts: Reflections on Sexuality and Spirituality" at the end of this book.

7. The same Greek word for "know" is used in Matthew 1:25 and Matthew 7:23; see also Genesis 4:1.

8. Bill McCartney with Dave Diles, *From Ashes to Glory* (Nashville: Thomas Nelson, 1995).

9. Luke 1:35.

10. Frederick Buechner, *Wishful Thinking* (San Francisco: Harper SanFrancisco, 1993), 119.

11. Philippians 3:7–10 *The Message*.

Afterthoughts: Reflections on Sexuality and Spirituality

1. Genesis 1:27.

2. Leanne Payne, *Crisis in Masculinity* (Grand Rapids: Baker Books, 1995), 86.

3. Matthew 6:9; see also Psalm 68:5 and Matthew 7:11.

4. Isaiah 66:13.

5. Matthew 1:25 and Matthew 7:23.

6. Frederick Buechner, *The Longing for Home* (San Francisco: HarperSanFrancisco, 1996), 23.

7. Dan B. Allender and Tremper Longman III, *Intimate Allies* (Wheaton, IL: Tyndale House, 1997), 234.

8. Ibid., 247–55.

9. I am indebted in this section to John Michael Talbot's book, *The Lover and the Beloved* (New York: Crossroad, 1985).

10. Song of Songs 1:15–16.

11. Song of Songs 4:16–5:1.

12. Mike Mason, *The Mystery of Marriage* (Portland, OR: Multnomah Press, 1985), 123–24.

13. Song of Songs 5:2.

14. Song of Songs 7:10–12.